Making Time for It All

Literacy instruction that is
comprehensive, high-quality,
and research-based

Kristi Cooper

Pembroke Publishers Limited

538 Hood Road
Markham, Ontario, Canada L3R 3K9
www.pembrokepublishers.com

Funded by the Government of Canada
Financé par le gouvernement du Canada | Canada

ONTARIO CREATES

Library and Archives Canada Cataloguing in Publication

Title: Making time for it all: literacy instruction that is comprehensive, high-quality, and research-based / Kristi Cooper.

Names: Cooper, Kristi, author.

Description: Includes bibliographical references and index.

Identifiers: Canadiana (print) 2025010301X | Canadiana (ebook) 20250103079 | ISBN 9781551383743 (softcover) | ISBN 9781551389721 (PDF)

Subjects: LCSH: Language arts (Elementary) | LCSH: Literacy programs. | LCSH: Lesson planning.

Classification: LCC LB1576 .C66 2025 | DDC 372.6/044—dc23

Editor: Kat Mototsune
Cover Design: John Zehethofer
Typesetting: JayTee Graphics Ltd.

Printed and bound in Canada
9 8 7 6 5 4 3 2 1

FSC
www.fsc.org
MIX
Paper | Supporting responsible forestry
FSC® C103567

Contents

Introduction

Making time for it all in a literacy classroom seems nearly impossible. It feels like pieces of literacy instruction are constantly being added to teachers' plates. When I began teaching, I knew I needed to prepare students to read and write. Teaching reading is overwhelming. Finding time for it all was a challenge, as there never seemed to be enough time in the day to teach all the necessary skills students needed to succeed in reading and writing.

Knowing why we teach what we teach is essential; however, we also need help with the how. Along with the myriad components of a rich literacy practice comes a list of best teaching practices. Universal design for learning, student-centred learning, voice and choice, and hands-on learning were added to the list of things teachers need to consider in their lessons. If that wasn't daunting enough, competency-based education and a new assessment format entered the scene. Doing all this while teaching real students with real and diverse needs seemed almost impossible. As a classroom teacher, finding ways to make time for all the essential components of instruction was challenging, often ending the day with a sense that some students, whether those needing extra support or those requiring extension, had been missed.

In 2010, I found myself in a dream role. An exceptional principal was concerned about our students' reading and writing scores. Many of our students were not meeting, or were minimally meeting, literacy expectations. The sheer number of students made it impossible to continue with traditional methods of literacy support. I was appointed K–7 Literacy Support Teacher for the school and was asked to brainstorm ways to support this growing number of at-risk students. This challenge, and my belief that the best interventions happen inside the classroom, birthed an idea for supporting literacy for all students while enhancing the professional learning of the teachers in our school.

My teaching partner Bryn was the Learning Assistance teacher for both English and French, and I was in the role of Literacy Support. Bryn was looking for ways to support a variety of literacy needs. Between the two of us, we brainstormed ways to better support the needs of all learners and to work toward a more inclusive, "push-in" model of support. After many long brainstorming sessions, we created a whole class literacy program grounded on the philosophy of *Love To, Learn To, Choose To*. This philosophy circles through the three phases continuously in a child's school career. Explicit instruction helps students learn the skills they need in order to read and to write, allowing them to learn to love and choose these skills as lifelong learners. Students inspired by their interests are engaged and motivated to want to learn new skills so that they can expand their knowledge and engage in information they are interested in.

Over the next few years, we created and refined our practice, working alongside excellent teachers and administrators. We saw enormous success as we changed how our school looked at literacy intervention and instruction. Trial and error helped shape the framework of literacy instruction that you will see in this book. The purpose of this book and this approach to teaching is straightforward: reading and writing instruction is most effective when targeted explicit instruction is combined with literacy stations. When students have time to practice, and teachers have time to meet with students individually, literacy flourishes.

Elementary teachers are everyday superheroes. Teaching young children to read and write, skills that unlock opportunities, broaden horizons, and transform lives, is an extraordinary challenge. This framework equips teachers with practical strategies to meet the diverse needs of all learners, ensuring that foundational reading and writing skills are explicitly taught and effectively practiced and learned. Many of the routines and lessons already happening in classrooms can seamlessly integrate into this framework. Rather than requiring a complete overhaul of existing practices, this approach offers simple yet powerful tweaks to maximize efficiency and differentiation. These adjustments ensure that students acquire the essential skills they need while freeing up valuable time for teachers to conference with students and address their individual needs.

A classroom where each student is known, their unique learning needs are met, and instruction is intentional and skill-focused creates an environment where everyone thrives. Students flourish as confident readers and writers, and teachers feel empowered, supported, and successful in managing the demands of their roles.

The framework outlined here is not just a roadmap; it's a toolkit for building classrooms where literacy is a joy, learning is purposeful, and every child has the opportunity to shine. You have the power to make a lasting difference in your students' lives, and this framework is here to help you do just that.

Acknowledgments

Land Acknowledgment

I am writing this from the traditional, ancestral, and unceded tmxʷúlaʔxʷ (land) of the Syilx / Okanagan people who have resided here since time immemorial. Much of who I am and what I have learned is a result of the land on which I have been fortunate enough to grow up. I am in a continual process of learning and relearning ways to join in the process of reconciliation.

Writing this book has been a journey down memory lane—reliving the moments and people who have shaped me both personally and professionally. It has been a gift to reflect on the learning that brought me to this point.

Many of the stories in this book centre around my parents. Growing up with them in my corner as my unwavering cheerleaders gave me the confidence to believe in myself. They taught me that hard work and kindness make life easier. I owe them a lifetime of gratitude for their constant support. To my mom and dad, Doug and Kathy Manning: your unconditional love and belief in me have been my foundation.

Much of my learning has also come from my three children. Each of them is incredibly different, and their journeys through school, learning unconventionally, have been some of my greatest lessons. To Alexis, Sam, and Nola: you will always be my greatest teachers, and being your mom is my greatest joy. To my granddaughter Georgia: I can't wait to watch you discover a love for learning and to introduce you to the magic of reading.

At the start of my career, I was fortunate to have incredible mentor teachers who shaped my perspective on teaching and learning. I am who I am as an educator because of the lessons I learned from watching them inspire students. Throughout my journey, I have been challenged, encouraged, and given space to explore by educators passionate about shaping the next generation of teachers. Words will never be enough to thank you, Joy Paquin, Fran Beckow, Maureen Dockendorf, Bryn Coape-Arnold, Jennifer Rowland, and Marion Barnes. Your encouragement and willingness to help me take risks and try new things form the foundation of this book.

To the staff at KCS: thank you for letting me experiment in your classrooms and for being my exemplars. Your grace as I learned alongside you, and your love for students and teaching, are evident in all you do. A special thanks to those who helped refine this book and shared examples of great classroom practice. Many of the stories of great educators come from my time working with you.

Finally, to my favorite cheerleader and champion, my husband Basil: your unending support and encouragement give me the confidence to take these risks. I couldn't do this without you.

1

From Research to Instruction

I entered the teaching profession at 21 years old. In my early years, I had insufficient time (or awareness) to examine the research behind my teaching practice. The first few years were about survival, as I attempted to integrate everything I had learned with the students in my classroom, all while trying to learn everything I could from the fantastic teachers around me. Rarely did I have time to delve deeper into teaching practice. At each professional development day, I would leave with new things I "should" be doing in my classroom. As an early adopter, I often implemented entire programs the weekend after a good professional development day. Never in my early years did I look at the *why* behind these practices. I just learned and leaped, taking any advice or experience and attempting to apply it to helping my students learn to read and write.

Observing student experiences in the classroom shaped my teaching philosophy and practice. I tried new things in a guess-and-test model and looked for results. I searched for new teacher resources to help grow my understanding of better ways to teach. While this resulted in many effective teaching practices, it wasn't until my graduate studies and a course on teaching literacy that I realized I had missed some foundational knowledge of how we learn to read and write. This research helped support my understanding of why I was making some of the decisions I was making in my classroom and helped guide my teaching instruction.

Research on Reading

Two key foundational models for literacy instruction are the Simple View of Reading (SVR) and the Reading Rope. The SVR, developed by Gough & Tunmer (1986), is a widely recognized framework that defines reading comprehension as the product of two essential components: decoding (the ability to translate words into sounds) and language comprehension (the ability to understand spoken language). Both elements are critical for reading comprehension, which is the point of reading.

In 2001, Scarborough built on this model by introducing the Reading Rope, which weaves the multiple strands of reading instruction together. The Reading Rope consists of two main sections: Word Recognition and Language Comprehension. Each of these components is broken down further:

- Word Recognition includes phonological awareness, decoding, and sight-word recognition.
- Language Comprehension includes background knowledge, vocabulary, language structures, verbal reasoning, and literacy knowledge.

As the strands weave together through explicit instruction and practice, a fluent, automatic reader with deep comprehension emerges. These models helped shape the skills that students need to be successful readers:

> Readers play a central role in making reading happen. In addition to acquiring necessary word-reading and language comprehension knowledge and skills, readers must learn to regulate themselves, actively coordinate the various processes and text elements necessary for successful reading, deploy strategies to ensure reading processes go smoothly, maintain motivation, and actively engage with text. (Duke & Cartwright, 2021)

The core of the AVR and *Love To, Learn To, Choose To* are the same. As Jen Kelly states in her book *Active Reading Classrooms* (2023), "Active self-regulation is essentially knowing how to learn and continuing to learn throughout one's life" (p. 11).

Students could have all the skills (decoding and/or comprehension) yet not be avid readers engaged in the reading process. The Active View of Reading (Duke & Cartwright, 2021), or AVR, addresses the issue of the student in the equation of reading instruction. Executive functioning, self-regulation, and motivation are essential components of the reading process. Additionally, there is an overlap between word recognition and language comprehension strategies that consider many aspects of the learner themselves (e.g. culture, prior knowledge). The Active View of Reading synthesizes the reading skills of decoding and comprehension and the student's motivation and engagement, illustrating the aspects of reading instruction teachers encounter in classrooms.

This comprehensive framework highlights the interplay between cognitive, social, emotional, and motivational factors in literacy development. It underscores that reading is not just about decoding and comprehension but also involves the learner's active participation in learning, blending insights from literacy and social-emotional learning research. The learner becomes part of the literacy model. The Active View of Reading model is the underpinning of this literacy framework, where the student is at the centre of the teaching.

Research on Writing

Like the Reading Rope, the Writing Rope (Sedita, 2022) provides a visual of the skills woven together into a cohesive model. The Writing Rope aligns with the Science of Reading and includes strands on Critical Thinking, Syntax, Text Structure, Transcription, Writing Craft, and the Writing Process. Modeled on Scarborough's Reading Rope, this model illustrates how all writing skills work together to form a strong writer.

Writing instruction has not received the same amount of research and attention in recent years as reading instruction. However, the article "Research-Based Writing Practices and the Common Core: Meta-analysis and Meta-synthesis" by Steve Graham, Karen R. Harris, and Tanya Santangelo (2015) is an analysis of the research into practices that are most effective for writing instruction. In this meta-analysis, the authors' research supports a focus on explicit skills teaching, as well as on engagement and motivation. Much of their synthesis reinforces the elements of effective writing instruction that have been most effective in my classroom. Effective writing instruction includes a positive writing environment, frequent opportunities to write, process-oriented instruction, explicit teaching of strategies, and collaborative writing opportunities (planning, editing, refining).

Building the Foundation of Instruction

Richard Allington's research in "Every Child, Every Day" (2012) addresses aspects of literacy learning that students need to engage in daily to grow as readers and writers. Allington advocates for students to engage in rich reading and writing activities daily across all subject areas. His research highlights that students who read and write more often (independently and with teacher support) develop lifelong literacy skills.

Every Child, Every Day needs to...

- Read something they choose
- Read accurately
- Read something they understand
- Write something personally meaningful
- Talk with peers about reading and writing
- Listen to a fluent adult read aloud

(Allington, 2012)

Keeping this in mind, an effective literacy program combines intentional, explicit instruction with well-designed literacy stations. A quality foundation for this program is essential for its success. The foundation rests firmly on three key principles:

1. Classroom Culture
2. Rich Literacy
3. Meaningful Assessment

With this firm foundation, you can build a framework where students can flourish.

Classroom Culture

Classroom culture is an imperative part of the foundation for literacy instruction. The students are the most essential ingredient in your classroom; knowing and building a relationship with them is key to a thriving culture. An environment where learning is a process (and mistakes are part of that process) and learning is active, fun, and celebrated creates a culture where learning can occur. Student agency and ownership (Guthrie and Wigfield, 2000, Zimmerman and Schunk, 2011) are crucial to creating an environment where students can flourish and learn.

At the beginning of my teaching career, I worked in a multi-aged Grade 1, 2, and 3 classroom with two exceptional veteran teachers. They team-taught and demonstrated the importance of inquiry, passion, and student-centred learning. Joy and Fran were experts at exciting learners, their love of learning was contagious, and being mentored by them was instrumental in shaping my teaching practice. Learning was everywhere in this classroom. Students were constantly engaged in rich learning opportunities, often without realizing it.

Joy and Fran knew how to discover their students' interests and integrate them into learning in the classroom. The classroom was filled with rich texts and inspiring items, encouraging students to read, write, and explore. Parents read with students in the mornings, creating a soft start to the day. Literacy was woven into every aspect of the curriculum, with units introduced through storybooks, poems, or songs. Students of all abilities were met where they were and inspired to grow. Joy was passionate about brain-based learning, teaching students the value of mistakes and risks, and building neuron "superhighways" (Politano & Paquin, 2000). Students were empowered to be active members of the learning community.

Learning happened everywhere you looked, and students were engaged and empowered. Classroom management seemed seamless, and the teachers made it look easy. It didn't take long to notice the intentionality behind their teaching. They worked tirelessly to create a classroom culture where students thrived. During my time with them, I tried to glean every bit of information from them I could; I was desperate to find the secret behind their success. I learned a few key pieces that I believe summed up their expertise.

Years later, I still hear Joy's voice reminding me to tell every student in the classroom quietly and secretly that they are your favorite. When students believe that, everything changes.

- Relationships Are Key

Students were seen and known. Joy and Fran spent the fall months learning students' interests, families, cultures, and skills. Students knew they were loved and known by the adults in the classroom. Mutual respect and kindness were foundational principles in the classroom routines. Students were treated respectfully, and the same was expected of them in return. As students understood that their teachers liked them, they worked hard to keep that respect and trust.

- Learning Is Fun

Joy and Fran were passionate learners, whose infectious enthusiasm inspired their students. Their curiosity and wonder about the world created a classroom culture that celebrated and encouraged student learning. New topics were introduced with energy and passion, and learning extended beyond the classroom into hallways and playgrounds. Reading and writing skills were taught using rich texts, vocabulary, and meaningful activities that made communication purposeful. Laughter and joy were central to the classroom, fostering an environment where no one took themselves too seriously.

- Learning Is a Process

Failing was embraced as part of learning, with mistakes highlighted and celebrated as opportunities for growth. The adults in the room modeled this mindset, showing that no one was perfect and that their mistakes were valuable learning moments. This fostered a culture where students felt safe to take risks in reading and writing, knowing their efforts would be supported and celebrated. Students understood that mistakes were a natural part of building a strong, resilient learning brain.

Classrooms are full of diversity. Creating a rich classroom environment involves considering all students in our classroom. The students' backgrounds and cultures are important parts of who they are. Considering students' diversity is an essential aspect of creating a classroom that supports the needs of all learners (Ladson-Billings, 1995). Some things to consider:

- Incorporating Diverse Texts: Can all students in your classroom see themselves and their families reflected in the chosen texts?

- Respecting Cultural Knowledge : What are some ways to incorporate students' heritage language into literacy lessons (morning messages, name games, welcome signs, writing activities)?
- Differentiating Instruction: What are the heritage languages of the students in your classroom, and how does that influence your literacy instruction? What are some assumptions you might make about literacy instruction that need to be re-evaluated through the lens of all learners?
- Building Strong Relationships: How can learning about students' interests, backgrounds, and cultures helps create safe places for learning?
- Equity in Assessment: How can we ensure that assessments are culturally sensitive and inclusive? When choosing texts or assessments, consider what prior knowledge (vocabulary, comprehension, cultural understandings) students might need to be successful. Look for ways to ensure that all students have equal access to success.

Teacher Tip
Be culturally responsive. Consider each student in your classroom and ask yourself if they can see themselves reflected in your classroom (culture, language, diversity). What could you add to ensure they can?

Rich Literacy

A favorite story to introduce reading and writing is *Ralph Tells a Story* by Abby Hanlon. It's a fantastic book that helps set the classroom tone by reminding students that stories are everywhere. Young readers and writers are motivated to learn when they understand the value of reading and writing. One key way to foster this in your classroom is by surrounding students with great texts.

Once, during a professional development workshop, a teacher boldly declared she could find a book for everyone to enjoy. I quickly adopted this approach with my students. When they said, "I hate reading," I would simply remind them that they hadn't met the right book yet. Filling classroom libraries with interesting texts doesn't have to be expensive.

When my teaching partner Bryn and I were building the library for the Lit Pit (the name we called our room for literacy stations), we found fascinating pamphlets from veterinarians' offices and regional parks (anywhere we could find interesting information). We grabbed them and added them to the classroom library if they looked intriguing. We would highlight new additions at the beginning of class: "If you love bugs and find facts fascinating, you'll love this new pamphlet on Black Widow spiders!" We scoured garage sales and asked families to donate old books. We also attended the library sale, where our regional library got rid of old books, and were the best customers at our school library. Our collection was built over time, and students were encouraged to bring and share books they had from home or the library.

It is important to pay attention to the cultures and heritages in your classroom. Texts that reflect many different cultures, heritages, and student identities help students see themselves in the stories in your room.

Access to various texts is imperative for students learning to read and write. Having a variety of books that are both decodable and accessible for students (they can use their decoding skills and reading skills to read them accurately), and books that are also engaging and culturally diverse, supports the different ways to enjoy and practice reading. Book areas can be divided into *Books I Can Read Accurately* and *Books to Read in Other Ways* (Burkins & Yates, 2021). Getting kids excited about different kinds of texts creates a culture where reading is exciting, engaging, and worth sharing.

Another aspect of a rich literacy classroom is read-alouds. Some of my earliest memories involve my parents reading to me, a privilege I now recognize as invaluable. Despite being a reluctant reader in my early years, listening to stories was a highlight of my day, even as a teenager when my dad read the *Little Women* books to me. There's something undeniably comforting about being read to.

Walking into a high school classroom with a children's book reminds me that the love of being read to never truly fades. Children's books are abundant and cover almost every topic imaginable. Reading them aloud can spark excitement about a theme and allow students to share their thoughts and interpretations.

Teacher Tip: Mentor Texts
Build a bridge with your school (or community) librarian. Utilizing their knowledge and expertise of great mentor texts and read-alouds can save you time and build your repertoire using great books.

Years ago, Faye Brownlie modeled a literacy lesson where she used the phrase, "Read it like a Reader, now read it like a Writer." This is an excellent reminder of the rich connection between reading and writing. Using mentor texts (any text that models a skill), students learn literacy skills by reading to decode, comprehend, and practice fluency, then shifting to writing to examine sentence structure, word choice, and story development.

Getting to Know You: Teaching Identity Mentor Texts

Hair Love by Matthew A. Cherry (Race, Culture)
Spaghetti in a Hot Dog Bun by Maria Dismondy (Culture, Race)
Red: A Crayon's Story by Michael Hall (Gender Identity, Learning)
What If We Were All the Same by C. M. Harris (Diversity)
Eyes that Kiss in the Corners by Joanna Ho (Race, Ethnicity, Culture)
Amazing Grace by Mary Hoffman (Culture, Ethnicity)
Not My Girl by Christy Jordan-Fenton and Margaret Pokiak-Fenton (Culture)
Under My Hijab by Hena Khan (Religion, Culture, Race)
Where Are You From? by Yamile Saied Méndez (Culture)
Sulwe by Lupita Nyong'o (Name)
We're All Wonders by R. J. Palacio (Ability, Diversity, Learning)
The Day You Begin by Jacqueline Woodson (Socio-economic, Ethnicity)

Artifact Bags

Read *The Matchbox Diary* by Paul Fleischman, highlighting how the small items each tell a story about the character's life. Show students items that represent you and your identity (culture, family, interests). Have students guess what these items tell about you. Ask students to bring a few small artifacts that represent them (their family, interests, culture, hobbies). Have the rest of the class ask questions about the artifacts, or draw conclusions about what the artifacts might tell about the student. Have younger students share what the items represent about their identity; older students write about their identity and what the artifacts represent.

Same, Same But Different

See page 16 for a Same, Same But Different template.

Read the story *Same, Same But Different* by Jenny Sue Kostecki-Shaw. Have students compare and contrast the two main characters using a Venn diagram. Then, pair students up and have them do the same activity with a partner, finding similarities and differences between them and their partner.

My Identity

Ask students to brainstorm what they think makes up an identity. Have them create a visual representation of the different things that make up their identity. They can use any visual representation they want to represent themselves.

Many Pieces of Me

See page 17 for Many Pieces of Me Template.

Design a six- to ten-piece jigsaw puzzle, with each piece showcasing a different part of your identity. For younger students, send the activity home so parents can help create the visuals to help show who their children are.

Who Is Your Name?

This lesson looks at honoring indigenous culture by saying, "Who is your name?" In Indigenous culture, your name honors your ancestors and the land. In nsyilxcən, language of the Okanagan-Syilx, your name is a *who* not a *what*, as it represents your connection to your background (people, places). When an elder asks, "Swit askwist?" you would share your genealogy and stories of your lineage based on your name that inform who you are. It also serves as a reminder that you are connected with others in this world and that you are not alone (Cohen & Chambers, 2016).

Create a visual with your name (and the pronunciation); see template on page 18. Include who your name is (your ancestors/ family and the land). Include your heritage and culture. Add your interests and hobbies. In the fifth box, add any other pieces of your identity that you would like to share. Younger students can do this with big buddies or take it home to be done with family.

Meaningful Assessment

Knowing your students' literacy skills involves assessing their abilities in key areas, such as phonics, phonological awareness, the alphabetic principle, reading comprehension, fluency, writing, and oral language. By identifying students' current skill levels, you can begin to tailor instruction to target specific areas for growth. This responsive approach allows educators to address both strengths and challenges, providing support that meets each learner where they are. Student data also includes information about the trends in your classroom, allowing you to craft meaningful, differentiated instruction that promotes progress across all literacy domains.

Assessment is an imperative part of literacy instruction, and early assessments in the year can help guide instruction. Many districts use different literacy screeners to assess students' literacy skills. The screener or assessment itself is less important than the assessed skills. If your district or area already uses a literacy screener, use that data to help drive your instruction.

Over the past years, assessment has been used for data collection to compare schools and teachers in many areas across North America. This practice has marginalized communities and alienated teachers. Data used for comparison and politics, or simply as busy work for teachers to meet district guidelines, has painted assessment with a dark brush. For our purposes, assessment is used purely to drive instruction and support student learning. The assessment is secondary to the data and information we gather about a student's reading and writing abilities. Additionally, the data we collect is used not for evaluative purposes (of teachers or students), but to drive and guide our literacy instruction. Assessment of literacy skills across a broad range of skills helps support individual and whole-class instruction (McMillan, 2010; Fuchs & Fuchs, 2006). See page 19 for the student self-assessment template My Reading/Writing Targets.

Literacy Screener: Skills to Assess

Kindergarten and Grade 1

- Alphabetic Knowledge
- Concepts of Print
- Phonological Awareness (describe skills)
- Phonemic Awareness (initial sounds, ending sounds)

- High-Frequency Words
- Listening Comprehension (K)
- Reading Comprehension (Grade 1)
- Reading Fluency (end of K–Grade 1)
- Writing
- Oral Language

Grades 2 and 3
- Phonemic Awareness (initial, medial, and ending sounds)
- High-Frequency Words
- Reading Comprehension
- Reading Fluency
- Writing
- Oral Language

Grades 4 and 5
- Reading Fluency
- Reading Comprehension
- Writing
- Oral Language

Keeping Track of It All

Once assessments are completed, creating a tracking document to keep track of specific literacy skills will help support classroom instruction. These tracking sheets and Class at a Glance documents are used only as a tool to help guide instruction and are never shared with students. For some teachers, this is best done digitally, whereas others prefer a binder with student tracking sheets.

The method of how you keep track needs to work for you and be something that is both accessible and manageable. Ideally, the tracking sheets would enable you to quickly access information about where each student is with respect to specific literacy skills (and allow you to add data to record their progress). In the upper grades, tracking students' reading and writing goals all in one place makes the Time with Teacher literacy station more streamlined and organized. Looking at the data from individual students allows you to start shaping student goals and identify places to support students in individual or small-group instruction.

Collating student data on a single sheet for decoding skills, reading, and writing allows for a quick overview of classroom trends. Viewing the data from a whole-class perspective helps identify gaps in learning or areas of collective proficiency. This information is invaluable for determining the skills to target in whole-class instruction, and for guiding focused support in small group instruction.

Once the literacy skills to be assessed (often tied to your district's curriculum or learning standards) are prioritized, a Class at a Glance document can be created; see pages 20–22 for templates. A common proficiency scale—Emerging, Developing, Proficient, and Extending—offers an effective framework for visually organizing student skills. This approach provides valuable insights into each student's abilities, guiding small-group instruction and individual explicit skill teaching. Additionally, the Class at a Glance document highlights trends in skill development across the classroom, helping to identify areas that may require focused instruction.

Same, Same But Different

Name: ______________________________ Date: ____________________

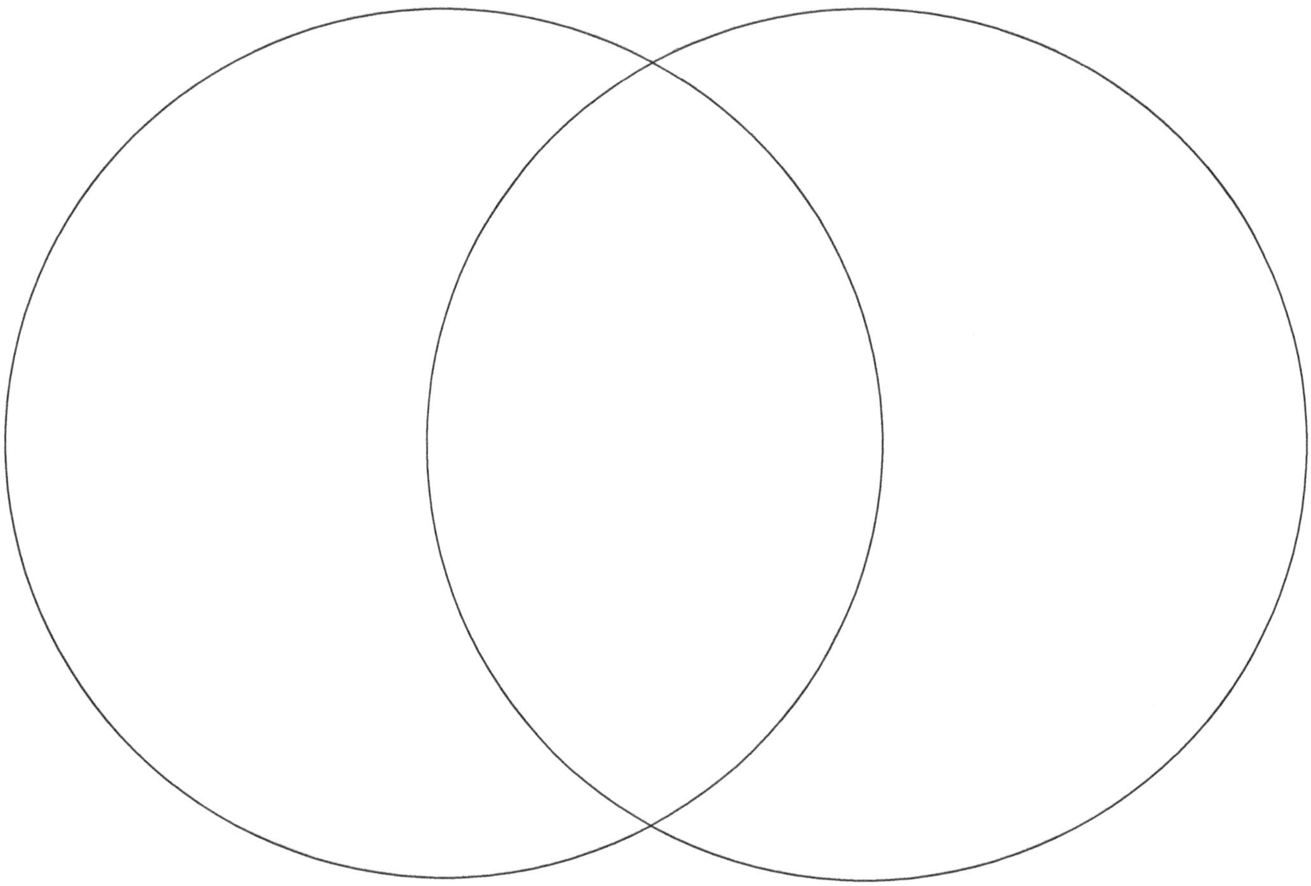

Pembroke Publishers ©2025 *Making Time for It All* by Kristi Cooper ISBN 978-1-55138-374-3

Many Pieces of Me

Name: ______________________________ Date: ____________________

Pembroke Publishers ©2025 *Making Time for It All* by Kristi Cooper ISBN 978-1-55138-374-3

Who Is Your Name?

<table>
<tr><td colspan="2">Heritage/Culture</td><td rowspan="2">Interests/Hobbies</td></tr>
<tr><td rowspan="2">Family/People</td><td>Name</td></tr>
<tr><td colspan="2"></td></tr>
</table>

Pembroke Publishers ©2025 *Making Time for It All* by Kristi Cooper ISBN 978-1-55138-374-3

My Reading/Writing Targets

Name: ______________________________ Date: ____________________

Learning Target	Start Date	End Date
I can…		
I can…		
I can…		
I can…		
I can…		
I can…		
I can…		
I can…		
I can…		
I can…		
I can…		

Class at a Glance: Writing				
Standards	**Emerging**	**Developing**	**Proficient**	**Extending**
Meaning				
Style				
Form/ Organization				
Conventions				
Editing				

Pembroke Publishers ©2025 *Making Time for It All* by Kristi Cooper ISBN 978-1-55138-374-3

Class at a Glance: Reading				
Standards	**Emerging**	**Developing**	**Proficient**	**Extending**
Reads Fluently at Grade Level				
Decoding Strategies				
Reading Comprehension				
High-Frequency Words/ Phonemic Awareness				

Class at a Glance: Early Learning Profile				
Standards	**Emerging**	**Developing**	**Proficient**	**Extending**
Alphabet Knowledge (Name, Sound)				
Phonemic Awareness				
Phonological Awareness				
Concepts of Print				
High-Frequency Words				

2

Designing Instruction

One of the challenges in teaching literacy is determining exactly what to teach. Overwhelmed by the vast number of skills students need to learn to read and write, teachers often turn to programs and resources for structure. However, without a clear purpose, activities and materials often lack focus and alignment with learning goals. Additionally, the skills you teach, and the scope and sequence of those skills, should be research-based. An effective literacy program requires clearly defined instructional objectives and intended outcomes for students.

Developing a scope and sequence for literacy skills and targets requires some upfront planning, but it is well worth the effort. While local curricula may provide guidance, they are often vague and lack the detailed specificity needed for literacy instruction. In such cases, online resources can offer valuable direction. Collaboration with colleagues teaching the same grade can be especially useful for identifying essential skills that require explicit instruction at each grade level. Clearly defining these skills streamlines the planning process and ensures effective and intentional teaching and practice.

Once the skills to be taught are clearly identified, activities can be designed or selected to teach and practice these skills effectively. Combining skills within activities and integrating literacy across subject areas allows for better use of time and ensures literacy skills are woven seamlessly throughout the curriculum.

One of the greatest mistakes early in a teaching career is assuming students know how to do tasks without explicit instruction. Many of the activities from online resources or teacher books are often fun and engaging; however, the intended learning outcomes are not always clearly defined. Reflecting on the specific skills students need to develop for success is frequently overlooked. Without proper instruction, placing activities in literacy stations can result in frustration, as much of the time is spent clarifying expectations rather than engaging in meaningful learning.

I Do, We Do, You Do

The *Gradual Release of Responsibility* model, introduced by Pearson & Gallagher in 1983, offers a structured approach to teaching. Their *I Do, We Do, You Do* model of instruction provides a structure that is both supportive and modeled. When introducing a new reading or writing skill in literacy, begin by modeling the skill to the whole class. Then, students can practice the skill in guided practice, supported by the teacher, with frequent check-ins to ensure that they are on the right track. Next, students will transition to independent practice, where they can practice the skill individually. During independent practice in literacy stations, students can practice the skill using text or words that are instructional to them. This model of instruction ensures that, when students practice these skills during literacy stations, they are familiar with the structure and comfortable with the activity or skill because they have practiced it before.

Many programs sold to teachers are presented as one-size-fits-all solutions to pedagogical challenges. However, these approaches frequently require adaptation to meet the needs of students, individual teaching styles, and classroom dynamics. The options suggested in this book offer a flexible structure that can be customized to fit various classroom settings and instructional goals.

Educators are unique in their methods and comfort levels within their classrooms. When I began my work coaching teachers, I believed (naively) that the way I was promoting classroom instruction was the correct one. My perspective shifted after observing an exceptional Grade 2 teacher whose approach differed significantly from my more-structured style. Her classroom thrives on engagement, energy, and the controlled chaos of a "circus tent" environment—literally, as she transforms her room into a circus tent for a day each year. Students are given more choices and flexibility, particularly during literacy stations, resulting in a vibrant, effective learning space.

Collaborating with her and other inspiring educators reinforced an important lesson: instructional frameworks must be adaptable to accommodate different teaching styles. Whether a teacher thrives in a lively "circus tent" environment or prefers the structure of clearly defined, sequential stations, both approaches can be equally effective in fostering student learning. The framework we are exploring in this book provides intentional, explicit, and systematic instruction in reading and writing skills, guided practice, and literacy stations that allow for differentiated instruction. It's also flexible enough for us to bring our unique personalities and teaching styles to the classroom. The key is to make it work for you and your students.

School districts and national reading panels across North America emphasize the importance of dedicating 90 to 120 minutes daily to early literacy instruction. However, covering all aspects of literacy within this timeframe can be challenging. While a 90-minute block may initially seem substantial, it quickly fills when essential skills require instruction and practice. This provides several options for structuring literacy time to best support teachers and students. A one-size-fits-all approach rarely meets the diverse needs of classrooms, as each teacher brings unique skills, experiences, and teaching styles.

Students can reflect on their learning at the end of each literacy station set and share with a partner or the whole class.

Each framework includes whole-class, intentional, targeted instruction that teaches systematic and explicit skills in reading and writing. Guided practice is where students practice the skills they have been taught with support, and literacy stations are where students independently practice the skills they have learned.

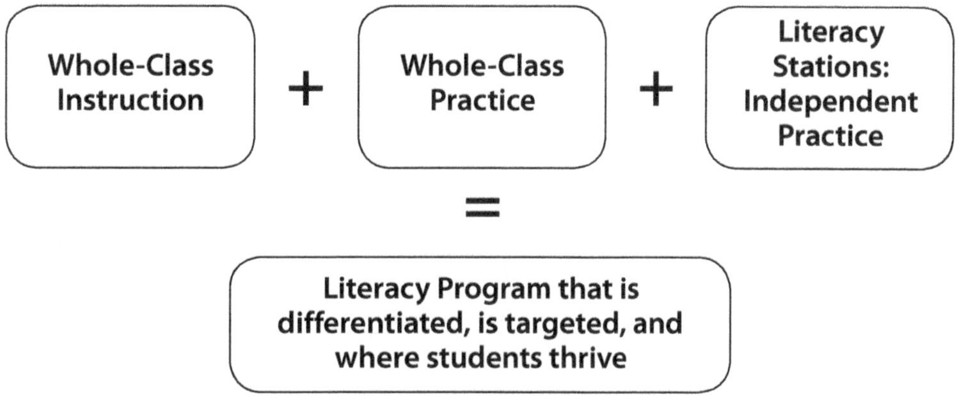

Teacher-Modeled Lessons with Guided Practice
Reading
Writing
Word Work (Alphabetic Knowledge, Phonological Awareness, Phonemic Awareness, High-Frequency Words, Vocabulary)

Literacy Stations	**Other Options**
Working with Words	Technology
Working with Text	Storytelling
Love to Read	Read to Partner
Love to Write	Listening to Reading
Time with Teacher	

Whole-Class Instruction

Literacy instruction in elementary classrooms is a topic many elementary educators are passionate about. Often, we include our own experiences in our classrooms, the programs that have worked for us, and our passionate opinions, and we hold dearly to our established classroom practice. Additionally, if you have been teaching for a few decades, you are unswayed by the "new" research or programs entering the educational scene. For many of us, our exposure to research was limited, and we explored things that worked in our classroom for our students.

Some educators lean heavily on whole-class teaching, and others on a station-based approach. This framework includes both. Research on literacy instruction has risen to the forefront again in the past few years, and out of that, the importance of explicit, systematic, intentional instruction has emerged (Kilpatrick, 2015). The Science of Reading highlights the importance of explicit instruction in foundational literacy skills, particularly for young learners, including phonemic awareness (understanding that spoken words are made up of individual sounds) and phonics (understanding that written symbols represent these words). There are two essential points to keep in mind when planning whole-class instruction:

- Whole-class instruction ensures that all students receive intentional instruction on necessary skills. Knowing the skills that your students need is an integral part of developing your literacy instruction.
- Whole-class instruction involves creating opportunities for skills to be differentiated and for students to be engaged in rich literacy instruction. These lessons are targeted and focused on a specific skill (reading, writing, and oral language).

The shift from activity-focused teaching to learning-focused teaching is essential.

In teaching, we often try to fit learning into a product or activity we have found. We are captivated by a great activity we see (or find) on social media or in a website or resource, and we teach it without knowing the point of the teaching. In this framework, your learning target or intention (the point of the teaching) is always the first consideration. Once you know where you are going, you can decide how to get there the (learning process) and how students will show what they know (the product).

Whole-Class Lesson Planning

Lesson design happens when we know the point of our teaching and then begin to develop how we will teach it to our students.

Unit	
Lesson Standard/Learning Target	What is the point of your lesson? What skills do you need students to learn?
Product	How will you know they know it?
Process	How will you introduce and teach the skill? Activate, Acquire, Apply
People (using Universal Design for Learning)	How can you meet the needs of all learners? What do you need to do proactively to support learners in your room?
Practice (Whole Class and Literacy Stations)	What will the students do to practice the skill?

The Point: What Is the Learning Standard or Lesson Target?

Many places have moved to standards-based assessment: for example, in my province (British Columbia), students from Kindergarten through Grade 9 are now assessed using specific learning standards instead of letter grades. In many places around the world, a focus on standards is emerging, and whether or not your district directs it, it is an easy way to help focus and refine your teaching lessons. When determining which standards and targets to teach, your priority is to look at your district's curriculum guidelines.

In our province, the BC curriculum provides guidance on which content and competencies must be taught at each grade level. After that, other instructional documents from your school or district can support the scope and sequence for creating learning targets for literacy instruction. Another important consideration is knowing where students are (more about assessment later), but this information is critical to helping design lessons.

A *learning standard* can be defined as a broad statement that describes what the student can do/know/understand at the end of a time of learning (unit, term). For example, *Students can plan and organize their writing, paying attention to the purpose and audience of the text.* A *learning or lesson target* is a smaller statement that describes what the student can do at the end of the lesson or a few lessons). For example; *I can identify the initial sounds in a Consonant, Vowel, Consonant (CVC) word, or I can identify the qualities of a main character.*

The Process: How Will I Teach the Skill?

Somewhere along the way, I picked up the words *Activate*, *Acquire*, and *Apply* to structure my thinking around lesson planning:

Activate: How will I introduce students to the new skill and get them excited about it?
Acquire: How will they get the information they need?
Apply: How will they show that they know it?

Activate is a reminder to me to think about how I will get students thinking and engaged in the lesson or learning I am about to introduce. In my teaching career, this has been critical to getting students to buy into the learning. Activating students' thinking can be done using a morning message, a mentor text, or a quick song or video introducing a skill. Students might come into the classroom to see activities set up that they can interact with for a short time before the lesson is introduced. A *provocation*—a collection of items, text, pictures that inspire and prompt students—is another excellent way of activating students' thinking and exciting them about the learning ahead, by introducing a topic and discovering (and building) background knowledge they might have about the topic.

Acquire refers to the way that the students learn a new skill. Teaching has shifted in many ways, and one of those ways is moving away from using solely teacher-driven instruction. Student-centred learning moves the ownership of the learning onto the students' plates and puts them at the centre. There are still (particularly in early years) many times when the teacher is driving the instruction. However, lesson planning can be an opportunity to look at alternative ways for the students to gain the skills they need or be more active in the process.

Apply is where students are able to demonstrate their understanding as related to a specific skill. Students can demonstrate their understanding in a variety of ways. Often, for small skills, this is a quick check-in to ensure student understanding. Students can also be given some freedom in how they want to show their learning. Voice and choice allow students to have some say about how their learning is shared. Formatively assessing where students are, and whether or not they have acquired the skill, gives you valuable information on student learning, as well as on whether or not you need to reinforce or re-teach the skill.

The Product: How Will Students Show They Know the Skill?

Examples of quick assessments are a Five-Finger Retell (see page 68) for comprehension, and Exit Ticket worksheets to check students' connections to text.

What the students do to show that they understand the learning target is often the area of focus for teachers. I loved thinking about the great activities my students could do to show their learning. However, I frequently over-emphasized the product and focused more on it and less on what the students were learning. The way that students show their understanding does not need to be a physical product. It is often easier on you, as the teacher, if the check-in is a quick assessment. This saves you valuable time, both in the assessment itself and in the preparation.

People: How Do I Support the Learners in my Classroom?

When I plan whole-class lessons and subsequent opportunities for students to practice the skill individually or in literacy stations, I consider the students in my classroom. *Universal Design for Learning* is a framework that considers the needs of the students in the classroom and proactively plans to ensure that the needs of all learners are met. After considering the point of the lesson and the process, I must consider the people in my classroom. Proactive planning—i.e., thinking about what students might need before the lesson is in full swing—is worth the upfront planning time. In the past, without these considerations, I was faced with "I don't know what to do" and "I'm done" comments. Adding this section into my lesson planning template allows me to ensure that I am considering any roadblocks of the lesson ahead of time, and attempting to plan for ways to ensure all students succeed and are supported.

Practice: What Will Students do to Practice the Skill?

Our classroom culture aims to help students see themselves as integral to the learning process. Students are empowered to become partners in their learning by setting personal goals based on where they are and what skills they need next in reading and writing. The belief that "practice makes progress" helps students recognize the value of consistent practice in developing new skills. Involving them in self-assessment and providing descriptive feedback also puts them in the driver's seat of their learning. When we are transparent about why they are learning specific skills and engage students in meaningful tasks, they are more motivated to practice. In our classrooms, students often encourage each other by saying, "Practice makes progress" when encountering challenges. Sometimes, when a student says, "I can't," other students will add, "Yet" to the statement, showing each other that learning takes patience and time. When goal-setting and self-reflection are modeled for them, students show incredible capability in setting goals and reflecting on their learning—two lifelong skills.

Practice itself needs to be modeled. When launching literacy stations with students, we must teach them the expected behaviors and explain why they are important. Returning to our shared learning commitments—"I will do my best to learn, and I will help others learn"—empowers students to see themselves as active participants in their practice and in supporting the practice of their classmates.

For many younger students, building stamina for engaging in tasks over extended periods is essential, and setting expectations they can successfully meet is important. Classroom organization and structure in the early primary years include building reading and writing stamina together, modeling expected behaviors, and creating classroom guidelines for effective practice.

When students see learning as a process rather than a destination, they begin to view the act of practice as a lifelong skill.

Encouraging students during practice means praising their effort rather than the final product. Students are more likely to stay motivated when we reinforce practice through specific praise. For example, statements like, "I love how Nola is showing perseverance with her word work this morning; she challenged herself with tough tasks and didn't give up," are more effective than saying, "Great job on your worksheet, Nola."

Making Groups for Literacy Stations

Teacher Tip
Avoid using terms like "low" and "high" when referring to groups, as they can undermine a growth mindset. Instead, use terms like "emerging" or "developing," which are less limiting and focus on progress rather than fixed capacity (Johnston, 2004).

In our first few years running literacy stations in a Kindergarten through Grade 7 school, we ran homogeneous groups based on reading level. We labeled them in colors and had all our emerging readers in our red group. Our reading groups were fluid, and we regularly adjusted the groups as each student progressed in their reading skills. Our color-coded system was our attempt to ensure students didn't know who was in the "low" group.

The homogeneous grouping of students was incredibly problematic. Often, our students who were emerging in their reading skills also were emerging in their executive functioning skills and motivation. Our red group struggled to self-start, and we frequently had difficulty managing their independent practice at each station. Alternatively, our purple group was composed of students who were extending in their reading ability, and they often flew through activities with ease. Students in this group were usually self-starters and enjoyed leadership opportunities. The similarity of this group and its homogeneous nature sometimes caused a clash because of personalities who were all looking to lead.

We invited critical friends to review our structure and provide feedback. One of the suggestions that was a game-changer was around our grouping structure. We were encouraged to look at heterogeneously grouping our students. This structure to group students (for teachers who would prefer structured groups over student choice) enabled us to group students who worked well together. These social groupings were intentional and no longer based on reading level. Instead, groupings were differentiated, balanced, and inclusive. Due to the heterogeneous groups, we could frequently change up groups based on need rather than reading level.

Once you have designed a clear framework for your literacy instruction (the *what*), you can design different pathways for achieving literacy outcomes (the *how*). A differentiated literacy program provides students with the opportunity to reach literacy goals in their own way.

The grouping of students in this manner created a need to ensure the activities were designed to be more open-ended (so that students were all doing similar activities), which prompted a shift in the activities themselves. Students working side by side, all working with different instructional level texts, created an opportunity to standardize the activity while differentiating the text.

Low Floor, High Ceiling

A few years ago, I began looking deeply into research on effective math instruction. In my role supporting teachers across grade levels and subjects, I felt underprepared in math pedagogy. I discovered two incredible educators and tried to absorb everything they wrote. Peter Liljedahl's *Building Thinking Classrooms in Mathematics: 14 Teaching Practices for Enhancing Learning* (2020) explores numeracy instruction through research, focusing on creating responsive, collaborative, and engaging classrooms. Liljedahl emphasizes rich tasks that encourage collaboration and deep thinking. Similarly, Jo Boaler's *Mathematical Mindsets* (2016) advocates for a growth mindset in math, highlighting Low Floor, High Ceiling (LFHC) tasks—problems with accessible entry points (low floor) and opportunities for complex exploration (high ceiling). These open-ended tasks foster collaboration and meaningful engagement. Boaler extends these ideas in *Limitless Mind* (2019), discussing how embracing mistakes, leveraging brain plasticity, and believing in one's potential can profoundly affect learning. Their research offers valuable insights for teaching not only math, but also all subjects.

I began to see applications of this thinking to literacy. In literacy, Low Floor, High Ceiling tasks provide accessible starting points for all students and extendable challenges for those seeking more depth. Open-ended literacy tasks foster collaborative, authentic learning experiences that worksheets rarely offer.

In classrooms of all ages, some students initially need extra support to start activities ("I don't understand") while others finish quickly ("I'm done"). LFHC tasks address this by offering activities with universal design, allowing all students to enter the task quickly while supporting limitless learning extensions. LFHC tasks promote inclusivity by offering a single, adaptable activity rather than separate differentiated tasks, which can feel isolating for students working on simpler assignments. High-ceiling tasks let students explore complexity, deepening learning without adding extra questions. With a shared activity for all, students feel included and empowered.

Creating LFHC tasks requires more upfront planning but saves time during student work. Thoughtful, universally accessible activities let teachers focus on individual goals rather than constantly responding to questions. Often, activities that teachers are already doing in their classrooms can be adjusted to become more open-ended. Worksheets found online can be edited to remove barriers and adjusted to create LFHC tasks. When activities are created open-ended so that they can be applied to various texts, teachers can differentiate for students by altering the text and not the activity. Students of all ability levels can use the same activity. The activity doesn't change; the text they are using for the activity does.

Students can also demonstrate learning in more open-ended ways than with limited question formats, like short-answer or multiple-choice comprehension questions. Instead of answering five multiple-choice questions about a text, students could show their knowledge in a graphic organizer that asks for the five main ideas. When focusing on character or story elements, students could use a graphic organizer that could apply to all stories instead of answering specific questions about a singular character.

Looking through the lens of Low-Floor, High-Ceiling allows you to begin to adjust and create differentiated learning opportunities for your students that can be used many times throughout the year, with the text changing, not the activity itself. Additionally, when students are working on the same activities, using different texts narrows the opportunity for comparison and provides opportunities for collaboration. LFHC tasks allow students to engage in the same activities using texts that are just right for them.

Recipe for a LFHC Literacy Task

- Know your Point: What do you want students to know and learn through this activity?
- Know your Students: What can your most emergent student do? What does your most extending student need?
- Evidence of Learning: How can students show what they know?
- Barriers: Are there any barriers to learning in this activity? How can you help remove the "I don't understand" and "I'm done" statements in learning activities?

Sample LFHC Lesson: Grade 2—Adjectives

Know Your Point	Identifying how adjectives help writers add interest and excitement to their writing and how adjectives help readers create pictures in their minds when they read.
Product	• Evidence of Learning: Reading Identify adjectives in your text and identify ways to help the reader visualize. • Evidence of Learning: Writing Identify places where adjectives could be added to your writing to add interest and excitement.
Know Your Students	My class has a wide range of reading abilities, and a few students are still working on emerging texts. Additionally, I have a couple of Grade 2 students who read and comprehend well beyond grade level.
Barrier	The adjectives activity that I previously used has adjectives that are difficult for my emerging students to read, but my extending readers often finish the activity quickly.
Process	• Students will use sticky notes to look for adjectives in their texts. When students find an adjective, they mark it with a sticky note. • Students who are emerging writers can indicate with a symbol how that adjective supported their reading (! for interest; an ear for helping them "hear" the word; an eye for creating a picture in their mind; a smile for imagining a taste; etc.). Students who can communicate their thinking in writing can record how the adjective helped their thinking while they read. • At the end of the activity, students can create an adjective wall or anchor chart and share their adjectives with a partner or with the class.

The Literacy Classroom

This framework is built on a strong foundation of classroom culture, access to rich literature, targeted assessment (understanding where students are to guide where they need to go), and an organizational structure. Its core relies on systematic, explicit instruction of reading and writing skills, supported by a gradual-release teaching model.

Students apply their learning in differentiated literacy stations designed to meet individual needs, while teachers use this time to work with individuals or small groups, conferencing and teaching essential skills. This framework provides a structure that supports all learners, ensuring they acquire the skills they need and have ample time to practice. It addresses the age-old teaching challenge: *How do I make time for it all?* by offering an efficient and effective solution.

Classroom Routines

In 2014, I heard a Ted Talk by Carol Dweck. Her "Power of Yet" (Dweck, 2014) and information on growth mindset drastically shifted my classroom practice.

Introducing the word *yet* into student vocabulary provided students with a reminder from our First Peoples Principles of Learning that learning takes patience and time (2006), and that learning is a process. Early in the school year, creating an environment that encourages students to make mistakes, see the value of *yet*, and be cheerleaders and champions for each other's learning is critical to a thriving classroom.

Setting classroom expectations and rules of behavior with your students can be a powerful tool in supporting the learning environment. Students are more invested when they have had input into the classroom routines (Zimmerman, 2002; Marzano & Marzano, 2003;). In our Lit Pit, we landed on two rules: *I will do my best* and *I will help others learn.* This became a simple reminder: Are you doing your best to learn? Are you helping others learn? Students knew that they were responsible for their learning and supporting the learning of the others around them. In my experience, when you give students ownership of the classroom culture, they are more likely to make it their own and take responsibility for their own (and their peers) learning.

Literacy To-Do List	
☐ Phonemic Awareness	← Differentiated
☐ Phonological Awareness	
☐ Reading Comprehension ☐ Writing Instruction	← Culturally Responsive
☐ Oral Language	
☐ Reading for Joy ☐ Writing Something Meaningful	← Social-Emotional Learning
☐ Reading Conferences	
☐ Writing Conferences	← Voice and Choice
☐ Read-Alouds	
☐ Systematic Explicit Instruction ☐ Assessment Of, For, and As Learning	← Student-Centred

Classroom Set-up

Setting the stage for literacy doesn't need to be complicated or to involve purchasing expensive materials and reorganizing your classroom. However, there are a few key aspects of your classroom organization that will make things a little easier.

Spaces for Literacy

- A book corner with comfy places to sit and access to many accessible texts for reading time.
- A bulletin board or trifold with writing prompts, word lists, and student exemplars for your writing station.

Table Groupings

- Desks or tables are set in groups so students can work together during literacy stations.

Books Books Books

- Books that are easily decodable for a variety of reading levels.
- A variety of books that are high interest and engaging for students, including books that students can read in other ways (Burkins & Yates, 2021).

Space for Time with Teacher

- A U-shaped or rainbow table; if you don't have one of these, a large table or space where you can work with small groups of students in close proximity is a good idea.

Anchor Charts

- Large chart paper displaying lessons you have taught your students that can cue students in their reading and writing strategies as they work
- Anchor charts that remind students of classroom expectations and commitments to learning that you can point to during literacy stations

Word/Sound Walls

- As high-frequency words and sounds are introduced, they are added to the wall for students to access during literacy stations and throughout the school day.
- The words on the word wall become non-negotiable words in the students' writing.

Editor's Checklist

- A list of the writing skills students have learned throughout their writing lessons. These skills are learned and expected in students' writing and are used as a checklist before students submit writing.

Literacy Stations

At the end of most teaching days in the classroom, there is often a lingering sense that the needs of the most emergent and extending learners had not been fully met. Shelley Moore refers to these students as the "outside pins" in bowling (Moore, 2019). Whole-class lessons frequently target the "centre pins," focusing on skills necessary for the majority of the class, but often overlook those who required additional support or further extension.

Literacy stations provide a structure to streamline the numerous skills students need to practice, including word work, comprehension, independent reading, and writing. This approach creates opportunities to meet with students individually or in small groups for intentional skill development. Implementing literacy stations can be transformative, even in the upper grades. The structure makes literacy time more efficient and allows valuable opportunities for student conferences—something that can be difficult to prioritize.

Literacy stations are simply a framework that provides a structure. Some instructions for implementing literacy stations are very prescriptive. This framework is a recipe that allows for substitutions and adaptations to best meet your and your students' needs.

The stations described in this book have emerged and grown, but they best meet the needs of a robust literacy program. They are simple, competency-based, and broad enough to be applied to various grades and content areas. Many teachers also include other options in their classroom literacy stations, and this framework is flexible enough to accommodate additions and modifications to best meet the needs of you, the educator, and your students.

Literacy Stations

- Working with Words
- Working with Text
- Love to Read
- Love to Write
- Time with Teacher

Rotation

When implementing literacy stations, teachers often ask: *How long should the stations last? How many rotations a day? Do students get a choice?* The answers depend on your teaching style and classroom needs. For those who prefer structure and order, a more controlled approach works best. If flexibility suits your style and students thrive in a fluid environment, a less-structured option may be better.

The key is to adapt the framework to fit both your teaching preferences and your students' needs. This might require adjustments as you go or even changes year-to-year, depending on your class. Some students might find a flexible, busier set-up overwhelming, so responsive teaching, modifying structure and support as needed, is essential for creating a successful and balanced learning environment.

Option One

Students are placed into station groups by their teacher, who keeps those groupings for several weeks (adjusting as needed). Students are scheduled into a rotation of stations chosen by the teacher, and the students have a set amount of time at each station before they tidy up and move on to the next one. Students are scheduled to practice skills at each station, usually twice weekly. Stations are scheduled three or four times per week, and students run through at least two stations (and reflection times) each day.

Things to Consider

- How long will each station run for?
- How will you build stamina to extend the time students can work independently?
- How will students know where to go next and which station to begin at?
- How will you keep track of materials for each student?

Things to Prepare

- a schedule for station rotations
- a visual schedule for students to reference
- places for each station
- a way to keep materials when students move from station to station
- anchor chart for expected behaviors
- stamina-building anchor chart (in younger years)

Option Two

Students are given flexibility in their chosen stations and are responsible for completing a set number of stations and tasks each week. When and where they go (and with whom) is the student's responsibility, and the teacher checks in during the week to see if the stations' practice has been completed. Station passports or magnets can help with the number of students at each station and keep track of where students have been.

Things to Consider

- How will you monitor the progress of student practice?
- How will you keep track of where students have been to ensure they have practice in all station areas?
- How will you manage behavior and noise?
- What do you do if many students want to be at the same station together?

Things to Prepare

- a visual map of the stations (possibly including maximum capacity)
- a tracking system for students
- materials storage for students to carry with them
- anchor chart for expected behaviors

Choosing Activities

With the increase of accessibility of learning activities online, it has become overwhelming and challenging to know what activities to choose for our students to offer them meaningful practice. This exponential increase of activities only adds to the difficulty, as there are so many options to choose from. When I began my career, choosing activities for my students was more straightforward, as it simply involved looking through a teacher resource book and copying what was there. Our options as teachers in the early 2000s were limited (which came with its challenges and benefits). Knowing the effectiveness of what makes a good activity can save you from choosing activities that don't serve your students or your purpose. Elements of an effective learning activity:

- Aligned with learning target or purpose: it reinforces the skill or learning that is taught explicitly in whole-class instruction. For example, reading text to find short and long vowels and sorting them to build an understanding of vowel patterns.
- Differentiated and flexible: it is adaptable for various skill levels in the classroom, allowing all students to engage meaningfully.
- Low Floor, High Ceiling (see page 29): for example, the text the students explore for their Word Hunt activity is differentiated according to their reading levels.
- Encourages application in context: it is connected to the reading and writing instruction and easily integrated into different subject or content areas. For example, the high-frequency words practiced in Working with Words translate into no-excuse words in the students' daily writing.
- Simple and manageable for teachers: it can be reused or repurposed for many different skills, allowing teachers to work smarter, not harder, and providing continuity for students (and involving less instruction if students already know what to do).

See page 103 for a sample of a yearly schedule for literacy instruction.

- Doesn't involve too much explanation or too many materials that can distract students from the learning itself; for example, Word Hunts and Sorts, for which teacher provides the context, and students sort words using their own differentiated text (long and short vowels, digraphs, nouns and adjectives, etc.)

Integrating Literacy

When learning is integrated, it is both more effective and more efficient. Learning does not happen in a silo, and other subjects can be seamlessly woven into your literacy framework. Enabling students to see cross-curricular connections between the disciplines by integrating your socials and science learning into your literacy stations can provide students with cross-curricular connections and build on their background knowledge of the subjects you are teaching.

Science, Social Studies, and Math do not need to be taught in isolation. Topics of study in each of these disciplines can be easily integrated into literacy mini-units and literacy stations. Cross-curricular learning allows students to practice literacy skills many times throughout the day. It also allows students to see the connections between the subject areas and the importance of learning to read and write.

Science and Literacy

Reading

- Use science-themed books for your whole-class lessons with students. Nonfiction texts can be great for teaching skills, such as synthesis, text features, main idea, supporting details, and checking for understanding.
- Promote texts tied to your Science topic. Encourage students to broaden their background knowledge by reading these books during the Love to Read literacy station.
- Choose instructional-level nonfiction texts for students to use when practicing skills in the Working with Text literacy station. Use these same texts when reading with students in Time with Teacher.

Writing

- Introduce writing skills, such as observations and text features, to the class during a whole-class lesson. Have students practice recording their observations. Using text features to support their writing is also a great lesson for your entire class.
- In Working with Words, have students do a word study on their texts and look for vocabulary words. When they find words they don't know, they can create definitions and build word cards that can go on a vocabulary wall or be taught to the rest of the students.
- In Love to Write, students can write observations, create how-to books with text features, or work on their research projects.

Science-Themed Mentor Texts

A Seed Is Sleepy by Dianna Hutts Aston
Ada Twist, Scientist by Andrea Beaty
The Tiny Seed by Eric Carle

Weeds Find a Way by Cindy Jenson-Elliot
Over and Under the Pond by Kate Messner
Water Is Water by Miranda Paul
The Lorax by Dr. Seuss
A Drop of Water: A Book of Science and Wonder by Walter Wick

Social Studies and Literacy

Reading

- Use primary evidence documents, historical text, and biographies for whole-group reading lessons. Integrate these into Working with Text activities.
- Use historical thinking concepts you have been teaching (significance, evidence, cause and consequence, continuity and change, ethical judgment, and perspective) as activities that students can do at Working with Text.
- Introduce books related to your Social Studies topic into your Love to Read station.

Writing

- As a whole-class lesson, teach a lesson on writing from different perspectives when looking at historical documents and discussing historical perspectives. During Love to Write, provide opportunities for students to write journal entries for a historical figure.
- When studying ethical judgment or cause and consequence with your students, encourage students to write persuasive articles or letters about social justice issues.

Socials-Themed Mentor Texts

Texts that celebrate diversity and are connected to heritage months are excellent ways of integrating social issues into your literacy learning. Using texts written by BIPOC authors and teaching students about social issues are effective ways of deepening student understanding of cultural, historical, and ethical issues.

The Name Jar by Yangsook Choi
Fatty Legs by Christy Jordan-Fenton and Margaret Pokiak-Fenton
Stolen Words by Melanie Florence
The Boy Who Harnessed the Wind by William Kamkwamba and Bryan Mealer
If You Lived Here: Houses of the World by Giles Laroche
I Dissent: Ruth Bader Ginsburg Makes Her Mark by Debbie Levy
One Plastic Bag: Isatou Ceesay and the Recycling Women of the Gambia by Miranda Paul
Malala's Magic Pencil by Malala Yousafzai

Math and Literacy

Reading

- Incorporate nonfiction texts or articles about mathematicians, real-world math, or STEM projects to inspire students' math interest.
- Show students how to analyze a math problem as a story to provide them with an opportunity to look at how the words in the math problem give them direction for how to solve the problem numerically.

- Read the problem together.
- Underline or highlight key details (numbers, operations, question words).
- Paraphrase the problem in simpler terms to ensure comprehension.

Writing

- Math Journals: students keep a math journal to keep track of their thoughts, challenges, and reflections. Students can explore their "mathattitude" and growth mindset.
- Writing Word Problems: students write and create their own math word problems connected to the skills you are learning in math.
- Math Vocabulary Wall: students keep track of and collect important math vocabulary and create an anchor chart to explain and define math words.
- Math Explanations: students can write the process in their own words to solve math problems or equations. Younger students can orally retell the process; older students can write a step-by-step process to help teach the skill to other students.

Math Mentor Texts

Mentor texts are a wonderful way of introducing new topics in math. Bridging the gap between numeracy and literacy by engaging students in books about math provides them with an opportunity to see this important connection.

The Boy Who Loved Math by Deborah Heiligman (about Paul Erdős)
Women Who Count: Honoring African American Women Mathematicians by Shelly Jones
Equal Shmequal by Virginia Kroll
How Big is a Foot? by Rolf Myller
Sir Cumference and the First Round Table by Cindy Neuschwander
How Much Is a Million? by David M. Schwartz (helps visualize large numbers)
Swirl by Swirl by Joyce Sidman

Monthly Social-Emotional/Cultural Themes and Literacy

Reading

- Provide books, articles, poems, and primary sources written by underrepresented voices.
- Ensure that classroom texts represent diversity and that all students can see themselves represented in the texts you teach and have available for students to read and learn from.
- Use history months as opportunities to highlight key authors and texts, celebrate different groups, and promote inclusion and equity.
- Teach whole-class lessons on the importance of knowing the author's story to help shape our understanding.
- Use multimodal texts—videos, songs, speeches, and artwork—to supplement reading and writing activities. Highlight the importance of oral storytelling, particularly in Indigenous culture, and emphasize it as an important and effective method.

Writing

- Highlight oral storytelling in whole-class instruction, using examples from local Indigenous groups (if storytelling is an important part of their culture). Have students practice telling stories.
- In Love to Write, introduce prompts connected to the issues you are introducing in class. Have students engage in reflective writing activities, answering questions tied to the texts you read as a whole class; e.g., *What challenges did that person face, and how did they overcome them? What are some ways our class can work together to celebrate our diversity? Create a poem about inclusion.*

Play-Based Literacy

Play is central to early literacy learning. Hands-on learning activities and opportunities to explore and use their imaginations are building blocks to essential literacy skills for students. "When children play and communicate through play, they are learning how language works and gaining an understanding of how to interact with other people" (Mielonen & Paterson, 2009). Learning and play are not in opposition to one another; the more integration students have, the more engaged they will be. Play-based teaching provides a meaningful and interactive way for children to build their literacy skills while honoring their developmental stages.

- Engagement through Choice and Exploration: Being active participants in their learning encourages students to explore language and literacy through playful contexts. For example, a pretend grocery store set-up allows students to read labels, write shopping lists, and engage in storytelling through role play.
- Development of Oral Language Skills: Interactive opportunities for students to develop their oral language and storytelling are foundational to early reading and writing skills. For example, puppets, plays, and storytelling allow students to practice their oral language skills.
- Authentic Contexts for Literacy Development: Play provides real-world contexts for students' reading and writing skills and embeds literacy into meaningful experiences. For example, students can create tickets to their plays in the writing station, create treasure maps for the story they are telling, and read signs and labels during their interactive play.
- Collaboration and Social Literacy: Group play fosters collaboration. Children can work together to build stories, solve problems, or create written projects. Social interactions during play focus on "creating inclusive, socially supportive environments" (BC Ministry of Education, 2023) where children learn literacy in a community with peers.

3

Working with Words

> "Reading should not be presented to children as a chore or duty. It should be offered to them as a precious gift."
> — Kate DiCamillo

Learning letters and sounds—and how they work together—unlocks the mystery of the written word. The ability to decode and encode opens access to a world that was once hidden. Teaching children to read and write is both a science and an art.

Working with Words provides students with opportunities to learn, practice, and play with words, building essential skills that unlock the world of reading and writing. These skills—such as phonemic awareness, letter recognition, vocabulary, high-frequency words, and parts of speech—work together to strengthen decoding abilities.

Two of my earliest school memories involve shame. The first involved spelling, and the second involved going to Learning Assistance (see page 93). I distinctly remember the dreaded Friday morning spelling test in Grade 1 and having to read our scores out loud. We traded our spelling tests with a partner, and they marked ours as our teacher read the answers aloud. I still feel the panic, knowing how much I struggled to spell.

Each time the teacher read the spelling of the words, my desk partner would look at me, and I could feel the heat rising in my cheeks. They, of course, got every word correct. I did not. Having to read my failing grade aloud to the class was mortifying. There were snickers and, in my memory, an audible sigh from the teacher. Week after week, the dreaded spelling test and my failing grades became a core memory and belief about myself as a literacy learner.

In my early days as a student, word work involved spelling tests and worksheets. The words rarely were connected to anything and certainly didn't follow any patterns. Words like *dinosaur* and *imagination* were found on the same list, and practice was word searches and writing the words in a sentence. Week after week, I would practice with my mom at the dining-room table, but on test day, the words would fall from my brain (and sometimes leak out of my eyes) as I tried desperately to remember. I'm not sure in which grade spelling tests ended for me, but these weekly tests did nothing to improve my spelling or understanding of how words worked.

You would think that, because of my terrible relationship with spelling tests, I would have avoided them in my teaching career. But, alas, I did not. In my first year of teaching, I was handed the spelling workbook for that grade (definitely one I, myself, had used in my elementary years), and off I went, testing spelling on Fridays. I had learned a few things and never made my students mark each other, and certainly never made them read the scores aloud; however, week after week, we trudged along. Truthfully, the spelling workbooks took the thinking out of this portion of my teaching. The spelling practice time was a nice reprieve and, most of the time, students dutifully alphabetized their spelling words and searched for them in a word search. I didn't need to think (and really, neither did they). However, I couldn't ignore the lack of progress in spelling within their writing. The same students consistently excelled while others continued to struggle.

A few years into my teaching career, professional development in Four Blocks Literacy transformed how I approached word work. Instead of disconnected spelling tests, I embraced the idea of making the words students worked on "no-excuse" words in their writing. These words, connected by families or patterns, weren't tested, but decoded and explored through activities like sorting and acting them out. They were added to a growing word wall that students used all year. For the first time, I saw significant improvements in their writing as they took responsibility for using these words correctly.

As my career progressed, I continued researching best literacy instruction practices. When working with teachers, word work often became a hot topic, as many teachers had programs or practices they were passionate about. I was unprepared for the controversy that would erupt when trying to work alongside teachers in the word work station. For some teachers, word work is an opportunity for students to practice activities from their spelling or literacy programs. Students cut, sorted, and glued words into families and patterns. For other teachers, this station was filled with fun ways to write words (rainbow, stamping, play clay), and although students were engaged and having a ton of fun, I wasn't sure that the work was growing their understanding of language or improving their reading and writing.

Ironically, literacy had become the area I spent most of my time thinking about and working on, yet I was ill-equipped and missing key pieces of knowledge about the actual building blocks of literacy. After a lot of mistakes and new learning about the importance of systematic, explicit instruction in the building blocks of language, I now know the importance of using the word work station intentionally as a practice of the skills and strategies taught in whole-class instruction.

Working with Words, for Kindergarten students, is a wonderful place to practice their alphabet, sounds, and phonological awareness skills. For early readers in Grades 1 and 2, word work becomes an opportunity to learn the building blocks of words and practice word families, phonemic awareness, and high-frequency words. In later grades, Working with Words is the ideal spot to develop a deeper understanding of the English language, build vocabulary skills, and practice conventions or parts of speech activities.

The Working with Words literacy station fits with a wide variety of phonics or word work programs already being used in classrooms. Alternatively, it can be independent practice for students to work on the skills they are learning in class. The activities themselves are not as important as the intention of the station, which is that students have the opportunity to practice the skills they are learning as a whole group. As well, they use the skills they are learning and apply them into reading text. As the students learn new words, sounds (phonemes or morphemes), or word families, these words are represented in their writing and are introduced as "no excuse" words (Ehri, 2022).

In the Classroom

On Monday, Mrs Hamilton welcomes her Grade 1 students into the classroom as they arrive. When they enter, she gives them a warm hello and a word that they then rhyme back to her. As Charlotte enters, Mrs Hamilton greets her and says, "Fish." Charlotte responds with "Wish." They smile at each other and Charlotte continues with some gentle start activities around the room.

When all her students have arrived, Mrs Hamilton welcomes them to join her on the carpet in front of the Morning Message. This morning's message is full of CVCe (Consonant–Verb–Consonent-*e*) words, as this was the focus of their learning last week. This message also introduces some *ea* words for students to practice.

Morning Message

Good Morning Class!

On Saturday, I went for a great walk and began to rake some leaves. What did you do on the weekend? This week will be so much fun! On Friday, we will make treats with our Grade 5 buddies. Yum! You will also get to read to them and eat the treats we made.

Today, we are learning about how kids around the world celebrate at this time of year.

I am very excited to learn with you this week.

As the students look at the message together, Mrs Hamilton asks students to come up and underline in blue the CVCe words in the message, sounding them out and practicing them in front of the group.

Mrs Hamilton asks if anyone notices a new vowel team in their message. She underlines all of the *ea* teams. Mrs Hamilton prompts the students to see if anyone can share what that vowel team does when they are together. She shares with the students that they will be building their knowledge this week by adding new vowel teams to the already giant list of words and sounds they know. Together, they read the message. They practice once by decoding the words they don't know how to read yet and then a second time for fluency and expression. Later, Mrs. Hamilton will use this message at the Working with Words station, where students will sort the words in the message into CVCe words and *ea* words from their list.

On Tuesday, during group work, they built words together after a small lesson on *ea* words. Small groups of students work on building *ea* words that they know by changing initial and final sounds. Students are celebrating as their lists grow. Mrs Hamilton circulates and listens as students build words together, helping prompt them when they come to a roadblock or read a word with a long sound when it should be a short sound. She stops the class and shows them how to use other clues to help their brains know which ones make sense. The Grade 1 students giggle as Mrs Hamilton talks about making her sandwich this morning on "breed." The students correct her and are proud of their learning.

During literacy stations, a group of students is doing the activity Going on a Word Hunt at the Working with Words station. The students search through different texts (independent reading levels) and find *ea* words. Once they have found and recorded their *ea* words, they share them with their table, building a giant word list. Partners at the table can assist students who are still emerging readers and need support sounding out words. Students who need extension and find their words quickly practice building other *ea* words that they know.

Throughout the week, Mrs Hamilton uses many opportunities to share other *ea* words and builds them into her read-alouds and lessons in other subject areas. Students are surrounded by literacy learning in everything they do.

Working with Words is intentional and differentiated practice of the essential building blocks of literacy skills that support students in developing critical skills for reading and writing, where students engage with the practice of decoding and encoding words. According to Ehri's research (2022) on the alphabetic principle, students progress through phases of word recognition as they build their understanding of the relationship between phonemes (sounds) and graphemes (letters).

Students in early primary (Kindergarten and early Grade 1) are in the *pre-alphabetic* phase, and can recognize familiar words, such as their names or environmental print (e.g., logos). However, they rely on visual cues rather than letter–sound knowledge. These students require explicit instruction and practice

- To learn letter shapes, names, and sounds.
- To develop an understanding of the phoneme–grapheme relationship (the connection between sounds and letters)

Once students have begun learning letter sounds and names, they transition to the *partial alphabetic phase*. At this stage, they start

- Segmenting words into phonemes
- Spelling and decoding simple words

Explicit instruction on the significant grapheme–phoneme correspondences is critical in this phase, alongside practice with high-frequency words and vocabulary building. Reading instructional and decodable texts during word work helps students apply their skills in context and make meaning from text.

As students enter the *full alphabetic phase*, they have learned most major grapheme–phoneme relationships and can decode and spell many words independently. Continued practice with reading and writing helps consolidate these skills. Instruction in this phase should focus on

- Expanding vocabulary knowledge
- Teaching the morphology of words, including root words, prefixes, and suffixes
- Deepening students' comprehension and word knowledge, enabling them to understand more complex texts

Lastly, in the *consolidated alphabetic phase*, students understand how words are structured and can recognize patterns within multisyllabic words. Instruction at this level should emphasize the following:

- Practice with multisyllabic words
- Building vocabulary through exposure to rich, varied texts

Whole-Class Instruction

Morning Message

Morning message is an excellent classroom activity to teach many reading and writing skills. This routine is also checks in on students' social and emotional needs and builds classroom culture. Morning messages can connect many curricular areas and units of study, and be used to model reading and writing skills. Working as a class to read the morning message supports students in learning what to do when they encounter words they don't know.

Teacher Tip
AI can be a supportive tool in writing Morning Messages that include many examples of words and skills students are learning

Morning Message Routine

Before students arrive, write a simple, welcoming message on the board. The message should be short (3–5 sentences for younger students and 5–7 sentences for older students), using words students are learning and focusing on specific skills like phonics skills, high-frequency words, or punctuation.

Sample Morning Message
Skill: Phonemic Awareness
Target: Digraphs: *th*

> Good morning, Grade 1!
> Today is Monday. Outside, the sun is warm. We will both play and read. Can you think of one thing you want to do outside? In Math today, we will look for patterns we find outside in the Fall. With our friends, we will learn about Thanksgiving. That will be fun. This is a great day to learn.

Working with Words Sample Lessons

In Working with Words, targeted lessons are intentionally quick and focused, often integrated into other teaching opportunities, such as the Morning Message. These lessons introduce students to new skills, which they then practice both orally and in writing. Many teachers rely on research-based programs that incorporate systematic and explicit phonics instruction, aligning well with the Working with Words approach. These programs often provide a clear scope and sequence, offering valuable support for early literacy development.

Working With Words Sample Lesson: Grades 1/2

Point	Digraphs: *sh* I can recognize and read words that have the *sh* sound at the beginning and end of a word, and use them in sentences.
Product	Student can recognize, read, and produce words with *sh* at the beginning and end of a word.
Process	Activate Mystery Sound: Picture cards on group tables that show words with *sh* at the beginning or end of the word (*ship, shop, fish, dish, shed, shelf, cash, splash*). Students share the words orally and see if they can discover the mystery sound. Acquire • *What sound do you think was our mystery sound?* Prompt students to answer, "S-H." */SH/ is called a digraph. It's where two letters work together to create a single sound. Let's see how this works.*

	Have two students stand up, one with the letter *S* and one with the letter *H*. *S says /s/ and H says /h/* *But digraphs are funny. When they are together, they don't say their individual sounds, they work together to create a new sound /sh/.* *Let's practice saying /sh/ together.* • */SH/ is very useful. It can come at the beginning of words.* Use the picture cards with /sh/ at the beginning and write the word *ship* with the students, decoding each sound as you go. You can use Elkonin boxes to show students how /sh/ lives together in one box, because it makes one sound. Prompt students to define what the word *ship* means, and provide an example of how it could be used in a sentence; or ask a student who would benefit from extension to come up with a sentence. *What are some other sh words that you can think of? Work together with your students to create a list of* sh *words.* • */SH/ also comes at the end of the word, like in the word* cash. Write the word *cash* together, writing out each sound, this time showing how /sh/ lives in the same box at the end of the word. Define the word *cash* with the students, explaining that it is another word for money, and use it together in a sentence. • Ask students other words they can think of that end in /sh/. If they are having a hard time coming up with words, use a word ladder or word chain to help, by changing either the initial or medial sound to make new words: e.g., *rush–rash–sash–dash–dish*. • Have students read a passage of writing together that has many /sh/ sounds. Shea has a shop. He sells shells and fish. A big ship stops at the shore to sell shells. A man shows Shea a shiny shell. Shea says, "I like this shell! I have cash." • Have students underline the /sh/, take turns sounding out the words and reading the sentences together. Make sure you define words students might not understand to build their vocabulary. Draw pictures to help support their learning.
People (UDL)	Emerging Learners: For students who are still working on letter sounds, create a word ladder or word chain that has some of the letters filled in. During practice time, check in with those learners and support them in using the sounds they do know to create /sh/ words. Extending Learners: Encourage students who need extension to write sentences for /sh/ words they enjoy. Can they write a sentence that helps their reader understand the meaning of the word?
Practice (Whole Class)	Have students create their own /sh/ words with either letter tiles or magnetic letters. Have them write them down in a word journal or on a white board.

Universal Design for Learning or UDL is an educational framework that focuses meeting the needs of all learners, through giving all learners a chance to succeed.

Practice (Literacy Station)	Working with Words Station: Students can continue building /sh/ words with letter tiles or magnets. Additionally they can work to find /sh/ words in their text. Working with Text Station: Students can first read decodable text that highlights the /sh/ sound. Next they can find /sh/ words in their instructional level texts.

Working With Words Sample Lesson: Grades 4/5

Point	Prefixes I can use prefixes to help me figure out the meaning of new words and understand what I read.
Product	Student will be able to identify a variety of prefixes and can use them to decode and comprehend new vocabulary.
Process	Activate Place words in prefix groups around the room. Have students try to determine what they think the prefix means based on the words in the list. Give students a practice example with the words *predict, prefix, presume, premeditate, preschool, premature.* Ask students what they think the word *pre* means and what it does to a word when it is the prefix. After students brainstorm, share (if they haven't gotten it already) that the word *pre* means "before." Explain that students will go and explore other words with prefixes and try to determine what the prefix means. Acquire • Bring students together. Introduce that a prefix—something that is attached (*fix*) before (*pre*) a word)—helps us understand the meaning of words while we read. • Have students look at the lists of words around the room (see page 50) and have them try to determine what the prefix means. Go through each of the lists. If students need extra support, provide the headings for them and have them match them. • Discuss with students that, over the course of the next unit, you will be looking at root words and at prefixes and suffixes to help you build your vocabulary. • Have students read a few sentences on the board: The unhappy student had to redo his homework because he made too many mistakes. She had to disable the autopilot before taking control of the plane. The scientist predicted that the microorganism would multiply quickly. • Ask students how prefixes help you understand the words and sentences better.
People (UDL)	Emerging Learners: Students who are not yet reading at grade level can be given words with *re–* and *un–*. Extending Learners: Provide students with a list of more difficult prefixes (see list on page 47) and have them find words (and meanings) for those prefixes.

Practice (Whole Class)	Apply Students can take the list of words they have learned and write the meanings for the words. Students can choose the words they want to define and write sentences for, and can be encouraged to choose words that are just right for them.
Practice (Literacy Station)	Apply Going on a Prefix Hunt: While students read their instructional-level texts, they will search for words that have prefixes and record them. Using those words, they will create lists of what they believe those words mean, based on the prefix, and then look up their favorite words for the actual definition. They will keep track of how knowing the prefixes helped them comprehend the text.
Add On	You can create a word wall that includes the root words, suffixes, and prefixes that you are learning as a class. Also, a vocab wall, where students gather great vocabulary, can be a wonderful addition to a classroom.

Prefix Lists

Means "foot"	Means "half" or "partial"	Means "self" or "by itself"
Pedestrian Pedestal Pedicure Pedal Pedometer	Semicircle Semisweet Semiprecious Semiformal	Autograph Automatic Autocracy Automobile Autonomous
Means "between" or "among"	Means "out" or "former"	Means "not" or "opposite of"
Interstate Intercom International Intersect Interview	Exit Expand Export Exhale Extract	Disapprove Disappoint Dislike Dishonest Disorder
Means "good"	Means "down" or "away"	Means "into" or "inward"
Beneficial Benefactor Benefit Benediction Benign	Decrease Decline Detach Depart Deprive	Introvert Introspection Introduction Introspect Introduce
Means "again"	Means "not" or "opposite" of	Extending Prefixes
Redo Reread Rewrite Retell Replay	Unhappy Undo Unkind Unlock Unfair	*Contra* means "against" *Circum* means "around," "about" *Intra* means "within" *Peri* means "around" *Retro* means "back," "backward"

Literacy Station

The point of the Working with Words literacy station is to practice the skills learned as a whole class and to help students develop a deeper understanding of how words convey meaning and support continued growth in literacy. Students can practice these skills in isolation and find these word patterns and phonemic skills in text. Engaging in word work inside text ensures that students can apply their learning to reading itself. Ehri's *Phases of Word Reading Development* (Ehri, 2022) highlights that connecting phonics and word recognition skills to meaningful reading tasks solidifies orthographic mapping, where students store word spelling, sound, and meaning in long-term memory. Without application and context, these connections may remain weak or unused.

Phases of Reading Development

- Alphabetic Knowledge: Lessons that focus on teaching students to recognize letter shapes, understand the names and sounds of letters, and connect letters to their sounds
- Phonemic Awareness: Lessons that develop the ability to manipulate sounds in words
- Phonics: Explicit teaching and skill development in decoding and encoding through word-building, matching sounds to letters, and identifying spelling patterns
- Morphology and Vocabulary: Exploring root words, prefixes, and suffixes to build word knowledge and deepen comprehension
- High-Frequency Words: Intentional teaching and exploring of high-frequency words, building students' repertoire through practice both in and out of the text

(based on Ehri, 2022)

A criticism of literacy stations for many teachers is how time-intensive they are. Teachers complain about the difficulty in finding meaningful activities for students to use in literacy stations. Everywhere you look online, there appear to be activities to photocopy to use with your students in literacy stations, except often they don't teach your students the skills they need to learn. One of the most significant ways to maximize your planning time and the efficiency of literacy stations is to use items in your classroom that you already have. Keeping it simple saves you time in planning and time in explaining things to your students.

Multi-Use Items

There are a few materials that are multi-use and can be used in many different ways, both in classroom instruction and for literacy stations.

Letter Tiles

Teacher Tip
Look for letter tiles with correct letter formation and where vowels are a different color.

Letter tiles or letter shapes can be used in every grade level from Kindergarten to Grade 7 (I'm sure I could find uses for them until Grade 12). Students can build words with them, sort them, and use them as prompts for word games.

Letter tiles provide a literacy manipulative that doesn't involve students having to cut out their letters. They are reusable and allow students to manually manipulate the letters (great for tactile practice). Letter tiles are great for word ladders when students simply change one letter to make a new word. Upper grades can draw multiple letters and create as many words as possible (no paper, no prep). Younger students can draw a letter from a pile and name as many words as possible that start with that letter. Letter tiles can be used in many different ways for many Low Floor, High Ceiling literacy tasks.

Little Items

Trinkets, such as tiny animals, miniature household items, or plastic food, can be used to create brilliant collections for Working with Words. These small objects are highly effective for sorting activities based on initial, ending, or medial sounds. They are often found in classrooms, family homes, and garage sales and make great literacy manipulatives. A large collection of these items reduces the need for printed pictures and offers excellent opportunities for LFHC (see page 29) activities; for example,

Kindergarten: Students can pick an item, identify its initial sound, and sort items by their initial sounds. They could also choose an item and brainstorm words that rhyme with it.
Grades 1 and 2: Students can sort items based on word patterns, sound out the words, and attempt to spell them.

Additionally, these tiny objects make excellent writing prompts. Students can select a few items and use them to write sentences or short stories. This approach is a versatile and engaging way to support phonics, vocabulary, and writing development.

Word Cards

High-frequency, vocabulary, or phonics pattern word cards are another item that can be used in multiple ways. Students can use them to sort, rhyme, or create sentences. They can also be used as practice for sight words. Students can pull a word card from the pile and try to find that word or find a word that comes from the same word family in their text.

Elkonin Boxes

An Elkonin Box is a graphic organizer used to support phonemic awareness and phonics skills by helping students segment words into their sounds (phonemes); see page 54 for templates for Elkonin Boxes. Each box represents a single sound, and students place a marker, letter, or object in each box to identify the corresponding sound in a word. Students love to drive cars into, or place small trinkets in, each box as they sound out the word. Elkonin boxes help students to listen and isolate the sounds in a word, as well as to connect the sounds to letters or letter combinations (graphemes). They are also great for helping students with encoding, ensuring that they break the words into phonemes. After practice with the whole class, Elkonin boxes can be used with letter tiles in literacy stations, supporting both decoding and encoding words.

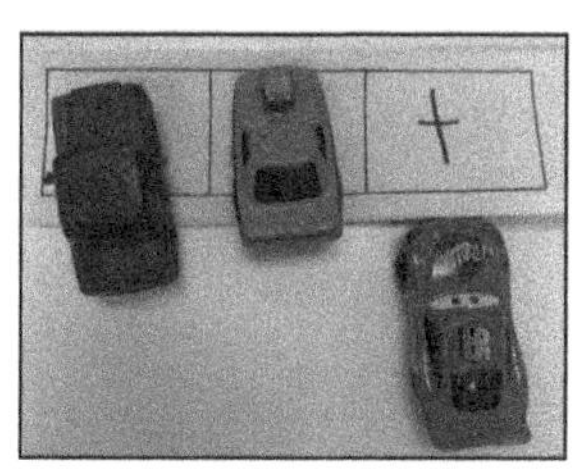

Activities

These activities can be used during whole-class instruction and seamlessly integrated into the Working with Words station. They foster active engagement and provide essential practice, ensuring that students build strong word recognition and decoding skills in an enjoyable and meaningful way.

Going on a Word Hunt

Create word cards tied to a specific pattern the students are learning and post them around the classroom or hallways.

Low Floor: Students travel around the room, finding and recording words that fit the pattern on their whiteboards or paper.

High Ceiling: Students can search their books for words that follow the pattern and record them and other words that they know

Sound Detective

Using pictures, word cards, or small items (see page 49), have students play I Spy but with sounds instead of objects: e.g., *I'm looking for something that has a "b" sound.*

Low Floor: Students use only sounds they have learned.

High Ceiling: Students use a variety of sound and word patterns to extend their learning with more than one rule; e.g., *I'm looking for something that has a middle sound that says "a" and is a CVCe word.*

Rhyming Word Challenge

From a set of pictures, word cards, or small items, students choose one and look for as many rhyming words as possible.

Low Floor: Students say the rhyming words.

High Ceiling: Students write the rhyming words, including multi-syllabic words and words that rhyme but are spelled differently.

Sounds Sort

Have students sort small items from around the classroom.

Low Floor: Provide students with categories to sort the items into; e.g., specific sounds (initial, medial, or ending) or different patterns (syllables, word patterns).

High Ceiling: Students sort the items into their own categories (related to phonemic awareness) and describe how they sorted them. They can show a partner their sorts and ask them to guess the rules they used.

What's in a Word?

Provide a large word (e.g., *elephant* or *snowflake*) and ask students to create as many smaller words as they can from its letters.

Low Floor: Use words with the letters and patterns the students have already learned.

High Ceiling: Allow students to choose their own letters and see how many words they can make.

Find It in a Book

Ask students to search through books at their reading level for sight words, phonics patterns, or high-frequency words.

LFHC: The text students use is the differentiating factor.

Sort It

Provide a mix of word cards and have students sort them.

Low Floor: Provide students with different categories (e.g., word families, blends, vowel patterns).

High Ceiling: Let students decide how to sort words (e.g., by sound, spelling, and meaning) and explain their reasoning.

Silly Sentence Builders

Provide a mix of word cards (nouns, verbs, adjectives, sight words). Students combine words to create silly sentences or short stories.

Low Floor: Provide students with only words they have learned in class.

High Ceiling: Ask students to augment their sentences with other words or structures to make them even better.

Word Exploration Journals

Students pick a word they find interesting, write it, explore its meaning, find rhyming words or synonyms, and create sentences or pictures.

Low Floor: Provide them with words using word patterns they know.

High Ceiling: Students choose the word and teach their word to the class.

Word Ladders

Students start with a word and then change one (or two) letters to make a new word. Each change creates a new word and supports students in thinking about spelling patterns and phonics.

Low Floor: Start with a word, and students change one letter at a time, recording the words they have made.

High Ceiling: Students start with a word and then create prompts tied to definitions for their partner. For example, starting with the word *cat*, students change one letter to make the word "you can drive it." Students can play around with how creative they can be with changing words.

Invent a Word

Give students common prefixes, suffixes, or root words and challenge them to invent new words and explain their meanings. For example, "What might *unflyable* mean?"

Low Floor: Choose a prefix or suffix that he students have already learned

High Ceiling: Students choose words that have new prefixes, suffixes, and root words.

What's the Word?

The word is *INCLUSIVE.*

Give students a mix of letters that contain a hidden word; for example, CSNIELVUI. Students can use letter tiles, magnets or even sticky notes with the letters written on them to try to find the hidden word, all while also trying to find as many other words using those letters.

Low Floor: Allow students to choose the mixed up word they want to try to solve. Students who are emerging can choose words that have fewer letters or letters they can easily combine to make words they know.

High Ceiling: Students can choose words that have more letters or more complicated combinations of letters to solve.

Reflection is an essential part of effective teaching and learning. At the end of chapters 3 to 7, you have opportunities to reflect on what you've read, your practice, and ways to move forward. Tweak, Toss, Treasure is a reflective practice for teachers, and it works great for kids as well.

Teacher Tweaks

Undoubtedly, you are already teaching some kind of word work or spelling program in your classroom. Ideally, you know the skills that you are teaching, and those skills follow some sort of scope and sequence. You also likely have a repertoire of activities you do with your students to practice these skills. An easy tweak is looking for ways to adjust these activities to create Low Floor, High Ceiling tasks and ways to remove barriers from the activities so they can meet both your most emergent learner and your student who needs extension. Another tweak is looking for opportunities for your students to apply those skills directly to the text. Having students work with words inside text demonstrates to them the purpose of learning these skills (i.e., so they can read and write).

Learning from My Mistakes

My mistakes in this station are vast. My lack of knowledge and understanding of the building blocks of literacy early in my career drastically affected the efficacy of this station. I had been raised in a world that dismissed phonics instruction and was ignorant of many of the skills students need to practice to support their reading and writing. I avoided teaching and practicing specific skills that I didn't feel equipped to teach (and had deemed unnecessary). As my research and understanding of literacy developed, I had to tweak many of my preconceived notions about reading and writing instruction. To reframe and adjust previously held beliefs is a challenging process. When working alongside teachers to develop their stations for Working with Words, I no longer focus on just "fun activities." Instead, I am intentional about building activities that match the instruction that is happening as a whole class and in small groups. Our practice is skills-based, deliberate, and based on explicit instruction.

When Bryn (my teaching partner in the Lit Pit) and I began developing activities for this station, we found a vast array online and quickly printed out an enormous variety of word work activities. We purchased letter stamps and wiki sticks, and found activities that involved the students rainbow writing the words, stamping the words, and building the words (among many others). While many of these activities were fun, they often lacked in transference of the practiced skills to the students' reading and writing. Additionally, the activities were not connected to the learning that was done in the rest of the class. The station (and accompanying lessons) lacked systematic and intentional instruction. Instead, our station included many busy-work worksheets that, although they were fun, were ineffective at improving students' reading and writing skills.

There is information overload when it comes to word work and phonics instruction. Millions of online activities claim to help students practice alphabet knowledge, high-frequency words, and phonemic awareness. Unfortunately, many of these activities are limited, lack differentiation, and are just busy work with little transference to student improvement. One of the greatest mistakes in my career was finding the activity I liked and not considering some key questions: *What do I want students to learn? How am I preparing them to understand it?* and, finally, *How will I know each child is successful?*

Proactively planning your whole-class lessons, by identifying the skills your students need to learn and matching activities to those skills, ensures your literacy stations are both engaging and purposeful. By starting with the end in mind and building from there, you can streamline your stations and teaching.

One critical mistake I made when designing activities for this station was overcomplicating them. Less is more when designing your station activities. Activities that seemed appealing with their cute clip art (yes, I'm aging myself!) often turned out to be narrow in focus and felt like busy work. Instead, aim for open-ended activities that are both purposeful and impactful for student learning. Many of the activities suggested here can be reused across multiple lessons and applied to a variety of skills. Creating LFHC tasks in Working with Words allows every student to engage meaningfully, regardless of their skill level, ensuring deeper learning for all.

Tweak/Toss/Treasure

Tweak

- What is a current practice or activity you are using in teaching word work that you could slightly alter to fit this framework? Is there an opportunity to adjust it to make the activity more differentiated? What belief do you have about word work that might need to be readjusted?

Toss

- What is not serving the learning of your students? What is too time intensive and could be made simpler in your word work activities?

Treasure

- What are you currently doing in your classroom that you love and that fits nicely into the structure of whole-class learning, group practice, and individual practice at a Working with Words station? What Working with Words activities are you currently doing that you can easily use at a station?

Elkonin Boxes

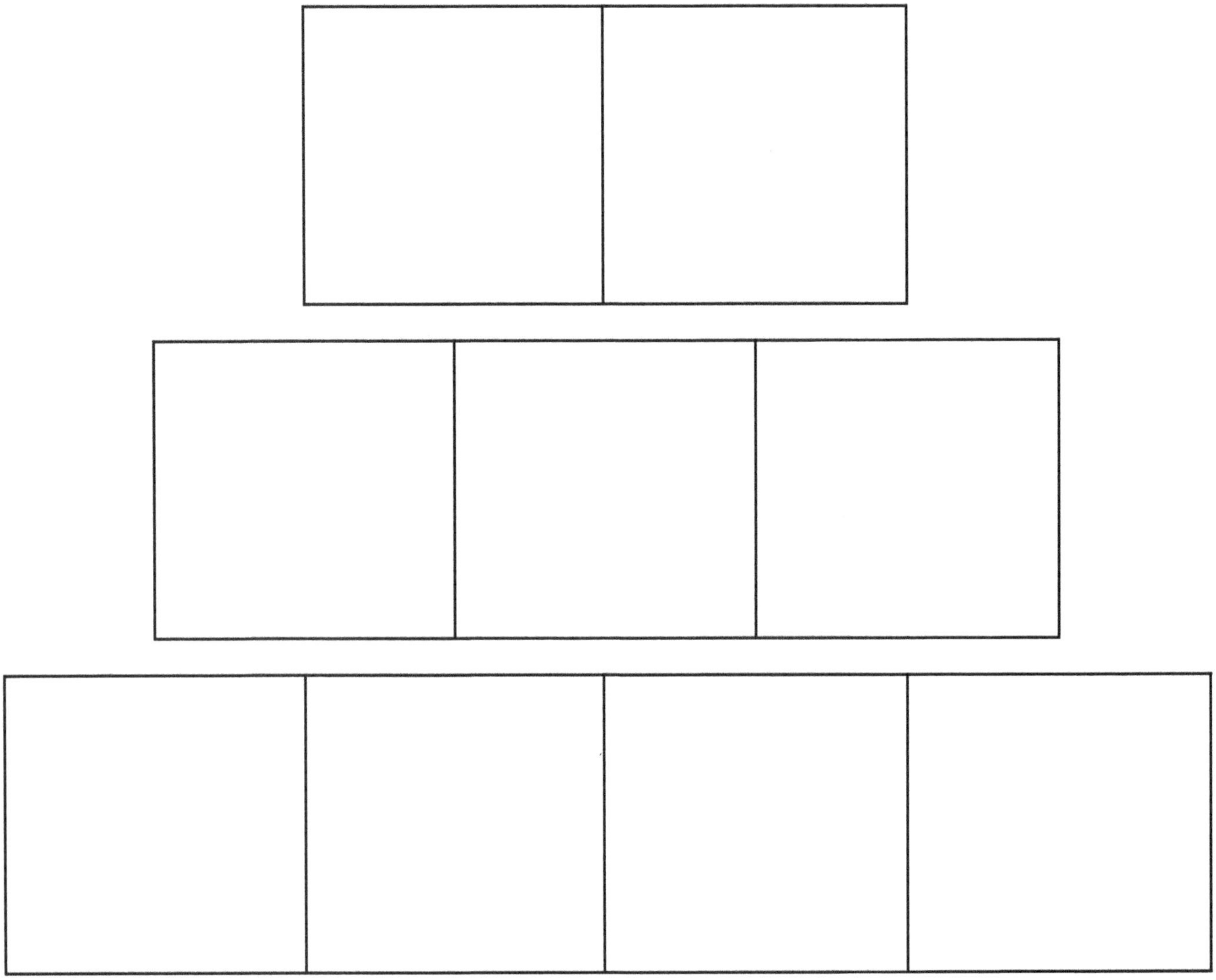

Pembroke Publishers ©2025 *Making Time for It All* by Kristi Cooper ISBN 978-1-55138-374-3

4

Working with Text

> "Reading is important, because if you can read, you can learn anything about everything and everything about anything."
> —Tomie dePaola

Decoding is just the first step—understanding what we read is another. Working with Text focuses on helping teachers teach reading comprehension through engaging lessons and structured practice in literacy stations. Too often, reading comprehension is reduced to answering questions in booklets. In this chapter, we'll explore strategies to make comprehension meaningful, allowing students to practice understanding what they read in texts that are just right for them.

I distinctly remember reading a class novel in Grade 4, *Owls in the Family* by Farley Mowat, a classic. Our teacher would read the chapter aloud, and we would follow along. This was a painful process for me, as someone who is easily distracted and doesn't always process well auditorily. At the end of each chapter, we would get a series of comprehension questions to answer about what we had "read." There were pages of multiple-choice and short-answer questions about the smallest details. I remember to this day that one of the questions was, *What color were the character's boots?* I think it sticks in my mind because I remember thinking (or possibly even screaming in my head), "*WHO CARES?*"

Reading comprehension questions often provide a lure of respite for teachers. They are pre-packaged and easy to find, and usually involve students busily completing the work. However, it rarely works that way in classroom practice. Inevitably, some students whizz through and finish quickly, and others need much support to read and answer the questions independently. Rarely do these sets of questions appear to support students' reading comprehension skills. Sure, some students can go back into the text and reread to find the answers, but it rarely involves the students learning how to think while they read.

The challenge is that our profession is incredibly challenging and complex, and sometimes a set of pre-packaged reading questions feels like a saving grace to reading instruction. When I taught Grade 6, I bought sets of questions for our novel studies and was grateful I didn't have to come up with much on my own. Yet I was left unsatisfied with students' skill development and still saw students struggling with reading comprehension. More questions, without instruction, didn't appear to support their learning. Fast finishers continued to finish fast, and reluctant readers did not improve their ability to comprehend what they read.

Fast forward to when Bryn and I were developing the Lit Pit, when our discussion around the struggle we both had with teaching comprehension became an area of frequent debate. We knew what we didn't want to do, yet we were unsure how to create literacy station activities for Kindergarten to Grade 7 and have them be meaningful and tied to their classroom learning. Working with Text was our response to a station that would allow students to practice reading comprehension. We began to create and brainstorm activities that were flexible and responsive, and that supported the comprehension skills students were learning in the classroom. Working with Text has continued to be refined (as all literacy stations have) over the years, but the spirit behind it remains the same.

In the Classroom

Ms Rowland's Grade 4 class sits crowded at her feet while she reads *Shi Shi Etko* by Nicola I. Campbell. They are engaged in listening to the story. Ms Rowland stops after each page and asks them to find words and phrases that help them create pictures in their mind. They talk about how the author uses rich, vivid language to describe all of senses in the story. With whiteboards on their laps, students keep track of rich vocabulary words and phrases. Ms. Rowland weaves in learning about the author's choices, but also the author's purpose, as the students are learning about local Indigenous groups and residential schools in their Social Studies. Students pay extra attention to how Shi Shi Etko collects items that help represent her and YaYa's memories as they extend this lesson into their Social Studies.

After the story ends, Ms Rowland draws columns with the five senses on the board. Students work together to fill the columns with the rich describing words used in the book. Ms Rowland asks the students to think about the author's purpose (an activity they have done before) and why the author chose to use such rich language when describing nature. Nola, a student in the class, connects their learning in Socials about how much their local Indigenous group values and treasures the land. The students discuss how the words the author has chosen to paint such a beautiful picture that, even if they didn't see the pictures, they could have created images in their minds.

Ms Rowland talks about how the words and phrases the author chooses help the reader to paint pictures in their mind and understand the story better. It adds both clarity and interest to the story. During recess, Ms Rowland prompts the students to pay attention to the language the author uses to describe nature. She reminds them to pay close attention to what they see, feel, and hear, and that they might want to use that as inspiration when they are at their Love to Write literacy station.

During literacy stations, Ms Rowland introduces the activity for Working With Text: the students will be reading in their text for words that help them visualize while they read. Students will use a whiteboard to keep track of the words and phrases, and then use symbols to help indicate which sense they are connected to. Nola is an extending reader and enjoys thinking about the text. She is reading *Pax* by Sara Pennypacker (which is at her instructional level) and records the words and phrases that create images in her mind while she reads. Basil, who is sitting beside her, is an emerging reader and is working on his text. Although the language is more straightforward and is at an instructional level for Basil, he can find many words that help him understand his text better.

> Throughout the next few weeks, the students will be working on a variety of comprehension strategies tied to their Social Studies unit. They will continue to apply their new learning to the activities in their Working With Text station. Ms Rowland is conscious about designing her lessons to include information about the local Indigenous group as texts the students use at the Working With Text station, helping support the students in building their background knowledge as well as helping them practice the comprehension skills they are learning in class.

Teacher Tip
AI can be a useful tool in helping differentiate text for your students. If you find a piece of text that you like, you can use AI to rewrite the text to meet the needs of different reading abilities. Use prompts, such as *Simplify this text by replacing difficult words with simpler ones suitable for a 2nd Grader* and *Rewrite this passage using basic vocabulary and sentence structure.* It might take a few tries as you reread the text to ensure it is accessible for your students; however, it can be a great starting place and a supportive technology when supporting learners of varying reading abilities.

Every child needs to read something they understand every day. Working with Text is an opportunity for students to engage meaningfully with text and practice the comprehension and thinking skills taught in class. Reading comprehension is the cornerstone of literacy instruction, allowing students to engage with, interpret, and critically analyze texts. Comprehension will enable students to engage with texts meaningfully, equipping them with the skills necessary to become lifelong learners. Reading comprehension is an active process and is woven into many aspects of the student's identity.

Background knowledge, culture, and vocabulary knowledge all play an essential role in reading comprehension. Over the years, the emphasis on reading comprehension has shifted. Explicit instruction of reading comprehension skills has replaced passive learning through exposure. In the 1980s and '90s, research around the gradual release model (Pearson & Gallagher, 1983) and the emphasis on meaning-making in text shed new light on the importance of explicit teaching of reading comprehension skills. The 2000s brought a renewed focus on the building blocks of word recognition. Linnea Ehri's research (2022) highlights how removing the cognitive load of word recognition leaves room for students to focus on comprehension.

In the 2010s, we saw entire educational curricula change and an enormous emphasis placed on higher-order thinking. Educational systems acknowledged that the arrival of the smartphone in the hands of students, and the exposure to the internet, came with a new set of skills that students now needed to learn (analysis, synthesis, and evaluation of evidence). Comprehension and higher-order thinking became even more critical as students required the skills to evaluate text and think critically and creatively about the excessive amounts of information they were exposed to. Out of this shift, we saw educators and researchers begin to focus on the importance of metacognitive strategies. Authors like Adrienne Gear, Jennifer Seravello, and Faye Brownlie supported teachers with ways to engage students in rich mentor texts and get them thinking about their thinking. Classrooms moved from students completing comprehension packets to discussions about ways to engage meaningfully with text.

As a relatively new teacher during these years of change, I purchased every teacher resource I could and began shifting my classrooms into thinking classrooms, full of mentor texts that we read and discussed. Comprehension became much more meaningful as we discussed different ways we can think about books. Bloom's Taxonomy of Higher Order Thinking began guiding my thinking about the different skills I wanted to teach my students, and I shifted comprehension beyond just regurgitation to meaningful engagement with rich texts.

Whole-class instruction and lessons became readily available, as many teacher resources provided wonderful activities and lessons to try. Yet this newfound focus on thinking and reading comprehension further added to the load I was feeling and my inability to find time for it all. I loved the literacy structure of the stations that I was using, but I found that most of them didn't include a station focused on reading comprehension. Working with Text was my response to my struggle to find time for it all. It became the place where students were able to independently practice comprehension strategies that we had learned in whole-group instruction, independently and in text that was differentiated for them.

Overcomplicating Working with Text activities can detract from the success of this station. We often try to overcomplicate practice with cute activities we find online. The easier and more open-ended the activity is, the better it will work at this station. This is the beauty of Low-Floor, High Ceiling tasks.

Engaging students in high-interest texts they can read is key to a successful Working with Text station. When choosing station activities, we often choose something that most of our students can do. In Working with Text, the activities are open-ended (Low Floor, High Ceiling), and the text students engage with is the differentiator. Students can work with books they are reading at their instructional level during Time with Teacher, or other books that the teacher chooses for them that each student can make meaning from. Students then use those books as their practice texts for the comprehension activities. For example, if the class is working on a main idea, the students can read their texts to find the main idea in their stories or texts. Students with various reading abilities can work in the same groups together on the same activity.

Whole-Class Instruction

Working with Text lessons are a great place to connect to other subject areas. Teaching comprehension skills like questioning or summarizing is easily integrated into different subject areas, effectively killing two birds with one stone. Any time I can incorporate activities, I am winning time.

There are many resources that provide teachers with options for whole-class instruction that support reading comprehension. There is no shortage of excellent educators connecting fabulous read-alouds to teaching students reading comprehension skills. As with any great idea, the importance isn't what lessons you choose; it's why you choose them. When finding great whole-class lessons, remember your first question is *Why am I teaching this, and what skills do I want the students to learn?* Starting with the why will enable you to connect your station activities at Working with Text with your whole-class lessons and ensure that you feel confident that you are teaching the skills your students need to learn.

Working with Text Through the School Year

Structuring literacy instruction around text genres provides an effective framework for organizing the year. This approach allows reading strategies to align with specific genres. In the Fall, focusing on narrative writing offers you valuable insights into your students, while emphasizing comprehension strategies such as making connections, exploring word choice, predicting, and checking for understanding. Integrating reading and writing strategies (e.g., reading as a reader and then as a writer) also makes it possible to use mentor texts that highlight classroom culture, social-emotional learning, and relationship-building.

During the winter months, the focus often shifts to nonfiction, integrating it with subjects like Science and Social Studies. Nonfiction comprehension strategies—such as activating prior knowledge, using KWL charts, identifying main ideas, analyzing text features, finding supporting details, and asking and answering questions—connect seamlessly to reading and writing instruction. These strategies can be practiced effectively in both Working with Text and Love to Write stations.

Spring is an excellent time to dive into fictional stories and poetry, which lend themselves to lessons on comprehension strategies, such as character, setting, plot, and literary elements.

Connecting whole-class lessons to one another and teaching them as strategies for both comprehension and writing saves time and reinforces skills through multiple forms of practice. For example, asking students to find words in their texts that help them create pictures in their mind, and then to use similar words in their own writing, reinforces the connection between reading and writing, deepening their understanding and skill development.

Suggested Working with Text Lessons

Kindergarten and Grade 1

Thinking While I Read Strategies

- I can make connections to the text.
- I can ask questions about what I am reading (or listening to).
- I can retell the beginning, middle, and end of a story.

Nonfiction

- I can identify the main idea.
- I can ask questions about the text.
- I can use text features and pictures to gather information.

Story Elements

- I can identify the characters in a story.
- I can identify the setting of a story.
- I can identify the problem in a story.

Poetry

- I can predict the rhyming word in a poem.
- I can identify words that rhyme in a poem or nursery rhyme I hear.

Grades 2 and 3

Thinking While I Read Strategies

- I can make connections from the text (to myself and to other texts).
- I can ask questions about what I am reading and find the answers in the text to help me understand it better.
- I can make predictions about what might happen next.
- I can summarize the key ideas of what I read (or listened to).
- I can identify the words the author uses to help me visualize.
- I can begin to make simple inferences while I read.
- I can use the words around an unfamiliar word to figure out what it means.

Nonfiction

- I can identify the main idea.
- I can identify supporting details.
- I can use text features to gather information.
- I can summarize information that I read.

Story Elements

- I can retell the main events of the story in the right order and include key details.
- I can identify the main and supporting characters in a story.
- I can identify the setting of a story.
- I can identify the problem and solution of the story's plot.

Poetry
- I can identify literary devices and how they add to the meaning.

Grades 4 and 5

Thinking While I Read Strategies
- I can combine information from different parts of the text to make new connections.
- I can make inferences by using clues from the text to understand things that aren't directly stated.
- I can recognize how the text is organized to help me understand the main ideas.
- I can determine why the author wrote the text and explain how the author's purpose influences the way the story is told or the information is presented.
- I can make predictions while I read.
- I can ask questions while I read that help deepen my understanding of the text.

Nonfiction
- I can summarize what I have read by picking out the most important details and putting them into my own words.
- I can evaluate the strength of the ideas or arguments in the text by considering the evidence and how it is presented.
- I can use text features (headings, diagrams, charts) to help me deepen my understanding of the text.

Story Elements
- I can evaluate the character traits of the characters in a story.
- I can identify the problem and solution in a story.
- I can identify the theme of a story or passage and explain how the author shows the theme through characters, events, and details.

Poetry
- I can recognize figurative language, such as metaphors or idioms, in the text and explain what they mean.
- I can identify literary devices and recognize how they add to the meaning.

Working with Text Sample Lessons

Working With Text Sample Lesson: Kindergarten/Grade 1

Point	Story Sequence: beginning, middle, and end I can determine the beginning, middle, and end in a piece of text.
Product	Students can identify the order and sequence of texts (what happened in the beginning, middle, and end).
Process	Activate • Introduce to students the idea of beginning, middle, and end. Ask students, *What happens at the beginning of our day?* We arrive at school. We have morning meeting… *What happens in the middle of our day?* We eat lunch. We have stations. We play with our friends.

	What happens at the end of our day? We have play time. We clean up. We get ready to go home. • Draw three boxes on chart paper. Explain that each box represents the beginning, middle, and end. Beginning: Where the story starts Middle: What happens next (the action) End: How the story finishes • Show students the front of the book, *The Very Hungry Caterpillar* by Eric Carle. Prompt students with predicting and background knowledge questions: *What you think the book is about? What do you know about caterpillars?* During Reading • Read the beginning of the story to the class. At the end of the beginning, pause and recap. Draw an egg and a caterpillar in the first box, explaining that this is the beginning of the story. • Read the next section of the story to the class. At the end of the middle section, draw some of the foods the caterpillar ate in the middle box, explaining that this is the action and it happened in the middle of the story. • Read the final section of the story to the class. At the end, talk about what happened at the end of the story and draw a butterfly in the last box. Acquire • Remind students that we are looking at beginning, middle, and end. • Above the first box, write the word *First*. Explain that *First* is describing what happens at the beginning of the story. • Write the word *Then* on top of the middle box. Explain that when we use *Then*, we are discussing what happens in the middle of the story. • Write the word *Last* on top of the final box. Share with students that *Last* describes what happened at the end of the story. • Prompt students to retell the story using the story boxes and the words *First*, *Then*, and *Last*. First, the caterpillar hatched from the egg. Then, the caterpillar ate a lot of food. Last, he became a butterfly.
People (UDL)	Emerging Learners: Provide students with a picture of a caterpillar egg, food, and a butterfly, and have them sequence the story. If they are able to do this, have them orally retell the story. Extending Learners: For students who are experimenting with writing, or who are already proficient writers, have them use the sentence starters *First*, *Then*, and *Last* to write the beginning, middle, and end of the story.

Practice (Whole Class)	Apply Give students the graphic organizer with three boxes. Have students draw their pictures in the beginning, middle, and end boxes. Encourage students to use those boxes to either write or retell the story, using the graphic organizer as a prompt. Invite a few students to share their work, using the words *First*, *Then*, and Last.
Practice (Literacy Station)	Apply Provide students with the same graphic organizer. Have them choose their own stories (or choose stories you have read as a class) and create their own beginning, middle, and end summaries. You can have emerging students use sticky notes to mark where they think the beginning, middle, and end is in stories that are instructional to them.
Add On	• Act out the story after you have read it as a class, to give the students a movement break. • At the Love to Write station, provide students with the graphic organizer to plan out their own writing. You can provide younger students with small items or loose parts and have them tell the story using those items, prompting them to use the words *First*, *Then*, and *Last* to show the beginning, middle, and end of their stories.

Working with Text Sample Lesson: Grade 4

Subject Areas: Literacy, Social Studies
Duration: 1 hour

Point	Visualizing and Author's Purpose Using *Shi Shi Etko* by Nicola I. Campbell
Product	Students will • Identify descriptive language and sensory details in *Shi Shi Etko* by Nicola I. Campbell • Analyze the author's purpose and discuss how word choice enhances meaning and imagery • Connect the story to their learning about local Indigenous groups and residential schools in Social Studies • Practice visualizing through reading, discussing, and recording sensory words • Extend their understanding by applying these strategies to independent reading texts
Process	Materials • *Shi Shi Etko* by Nicola I. Campbell • whiteboards and markers (one per student) • chart paper or whiteboard for group activity • students' independent reading texts for literacy stations 1. Introduction (10 minutes) • Gather students on the carpet. • Briefly explain the purpose of the lesson: *Today, we'll explore how authors use descriptive language to help us visualize while reading. We'll also connect this to our learning about Indigenous groups and their connection to the land.*

<table>
<tr><td></td><td>2. Read-Aloud and Guided Visualization (20 minutes)
• Read Shi Shi Etko aloud. Pause after each page and ask, What words or phrases help you create pictures in your mind? Which senses do these words appeal to?
• Student Engagement: Students record rich vocabulary and phrases on whiteboards as they listen. Discuss as a group, focusing on how sensory details enhance the story.
• Five Senses Chart: Draw five columns (one for each sense) on the board. Work as a class to categorize words and phrases from the story under the appropriate sense.

3. Author's Purpose Discussion (10 minutes)
• Prompt students to think about the author's purpose: Why do you think Nicola I. Campbell uses such rich language to describe nature? How does this connect to what we've learned about the local Indigenous group's connection to the land?
• Facilitate a discussion, encouraging connections between Social Studies learning and the story's themes.

4. Recess Extension (Outdoor Activity)
• Before recess, encourage students to observe their surroundings: Notice what you see, hear, and feel outside. How would you describe it to someone else using rich language? You might want to use this inspiration in our writing station later.

5. Literacy Stations: Working With Text (20 minutes)
Introduce the independent activity:
• Students read their own text and identify words and phrases that help them visualize.
• Students record the words and phrases on their whiteboards and use symbols to indicate the sense they appeal to.
Differentiation: Support Alex, an emerging reader, with a simpler text that matches her instructional level. Encourage Drew, an extending reader, to deepen his analysis by identifying patterns or themes.

6. Closing and Reflection (5 minutes)
• Gather students to share examples from their independent reading: Which words helped you visualize? Why do you think the author chose those words?
• Reinforce the connection between sensory language and understanding texts.</td></tr>
<tr><td>People (UDL)</td><td>• Provide scaffolded texts for emerging readers and additional challenges (e.g., thematic connections) for extending readers.
• Offer sentence stems or graphic organizers for students who need additional support identifying sensory details or the author's purpose.</td></tr>
<tr><td>Practice
(Whole Class)</td><td>Social Studies Integration: Extend the discussion to how Indigenous storytelling often incorporates a deep respect for nature and the land.</td></tr>
<tr><td>Practice
(Literacy Station)</td><td>Writing Connection: At the Love to Write station, students can use their sensory observations from recess to write a descriptive paragraph inspired by nature.</td></tr>
</table>

Assessment	• Observe student participation during the read-aloud and discussions. • Review students' recorded words and phrases during independent reading for comprehension and engagement with sensory language.
Reflection Notes (Post-Lesson)	• Did students engage effectively with the sensory details in the text? • Were they able to connect the author's purpose to their Social Studies learning? • How well did the independent reading activity reinforce the skills taught during the read-aloud?

Literacy Station

Comprehending what you read is the ultimate purpose of reading. Working with Text is a station where students can practice and strengthen their reading comprehension skills using texts that are just right for them.

In my role coaching teachers for the past nine years, I have had the luxury of working alongside excellent teachers willing to try different approaches with me. In our Working With Text stations, we have tried a lot of different activities and learned from our mistakes. A few activities have continued to rise to the top, as they both engage the students in learning and promote the practice of the skill. Ironically, these activities are the most simple.

Activities

Using Sticky Notes

Sticky Notes have been a game-changer in helping students practice their comprehension strategies. They are Low Floor, High Ceiling, and allow students to keep track of their thinking in text that they can decode. Students can read through their text and flag great words if they have just learned a lesson on word choice and words the author chooses to help the reader visualize. Recording those words on a sticky note allows you to choose some words to later define and learn as a class. These words can be added to an anchor chart or a vocabulary wall for students to refer back to (for their writing). Students in the upper years can find words that help them visualize and then create vocabulary cards, defining the word, using it in a sentence, and providing a reason that their peers should use this word in their writing. They can also explain how this word helped them understand the text they were reading and suggest why the author may have chosen it.

Famished – adjective
Definition – extremely hungry or starving
Sentence – After my basketball game, I was famished.
Use this word if – you are looking for a powerful word that expresses extreme hunger. It is an excellent replacement for the word *hungry* and is more appropriate than *starving*.

Sticky notes are also wonderful for helping students mark things like the main ideas or the climax of their story in their book.

Using Whiteboards

Whiteboards are another universal resource for all station activities. In Working with Text, students can use whiteboards to record questions, connections, or quotes (for upper grades) that help them make meaning. Simplifying the activity allows students to keep track of their thinking in low-stakes ways. Some whiteboard activities:

- I Connect: Students draw or write connections they have to the text they are reading.
- Who, What, When, Where: Students record or draw answers to simple prompts.
- Character Feelings: Students draw or write about the characters' feelings while they read.
- Retell: Students draw or write simple words to show what happens at the beginning, middle, and end of their text.
- Did You Know? Students write their questions while they read and then sort them into *thick* or *thin* questions.
- Word Collector: Students capture words that help make the text interesting as they read. Afterwards, they can sort the words into categories.
- Character Snapshot: Students create a map of the character's qualities while they read.
- Show, Don't Tell: Students record inferences they made while reading.

  I think ______ because _______.

Reflection is an essential part of effective teaching and learning. At the end of chapters 3 to 7, you have opportunities to reflect on what you've read, your practice, and ways to move forward. Tweak, Toss, Treasure is a reflective practice for teachers, and it works great for kids as well.

Teacher Tweaks

Many of the comprehension activities you are already doing in your classroom can be adjusted to create Low Floor, High Ceiling tasks. Your character diagram for specific mentor texts or novel studies can be adjusted to become a character activity that can be used for all kinds of texts. Instead of answering pages of comprehension questions, you can have students record questions that they have while they read and have their partners see if they can answer them. Comprehension questions can also be modified and replaced with activities that still serve the same purpose but are focused on key themes (e.g., an idea, character, setting, text features, conflict/resolution).

Learning from My Mistakes

In my first year of Working with Text, I found great open-ended activities for the students to do. Unfortunately, I had not modeled how to do these activities as a whole class. When students arrived at their stations, they struggled to understand what to do, and I was left running over and reactively explaining the process.

The most epic fail was our attempt at interactive notebooks, where the students had to cut out papers and glue them into their notebooks. The majority of the literacy block was spent dealing with scissors and glue and the ensuing mess. A good rule of thumb I learned after this: if the preparation for the activity takes more time than the activity itself, ditch it.

Lastly, and likely my biggest mistake, was making the activities far too complicated. Working with Text is an excellent opportunity for students to engage with the text and practice various comprehension skills and strategies. Finding the main idea does not need to involve a beautiful worksheet; it can be as simple as recording it on a whiteboard. Keeping things simple and focusing on the point of the practice simplified and streamlined this station, and it meant that students could focus their learning as well.

Tweak/Toss/Treasure

Tweak

- What is a current practice or activity you are using in teaching reading comprehension that you could slightly alter to fit this framework? Is there an opportunity to adjust it to make the activity more differentiated? What belief do you have about reading comprehension that may need to be readjusted?

Toss

- What is not serving the learning of your students? What is too time-intensive and could be made simpler in your comprehension activities?

Treasure

- What are you currently doing in your classroom that you love and that fits nicely into the structure of whole-class learning, group practice, and individual practice at a Working with Text station? What comprehension activities are you currently doing that you can easily use at a station?

5

Independent Reading

"To learn to read is to light a fire."
— Victor Hugo, *Les Miserables*

Inspiring a love of reading is no small feat, especially in a generation filled with distractions. This chapter outlines classroom routines, structures, and lessons to help foster a love of reading and integrate this into your literacy station routines. This approach creates space in the timetable while still providing valuable opportunities for students to read for enjoyment.

Richard Allington highlighted the importance of every child reading for choice, as one of the things good readers need to do every day. The Active Reading model also highlights motivation and engagement as essential for students learning to read. Story can be a source of creativity and joy. In my experience, when students catch the bug of reading and find something they enjoy reading or are interested in, they are motivated to choose and practice it.

Reading something they choose promotes student engagement in the reading process itself. This ties directly to my teaching philosophy of Love To, Learn To, and Choose To: when students love it, they will be motivated to learn it and hopefully choose it as lifelong learners.

Scarborough's Reading Rope (2001) provides clarity on the skills embedded in literacy instruction. Word recognition and language comprehension skills (and their component parts) must be explicitly taught in whole-class instruction. In the older grades, reading comprehension, vocabulary, fluency, and expression are also skills that must be explicitly taught. In the Active View Of Reading (Duke & Cartwright, 2021), a key aspect of reading is student self-regulation. Critical components like motivation, engagement, and executive functioning are considered integral aspects of a student's ability to learn to read.

In elementary and high school, silent reading used to be a regular practice. I fondly remember the thirty to forty minutes after lunch when we would all take out a book and "read." In my early years in elementary school, when I was still a reluctant reader, this block of time was centuries long. I would grab a book and my eyes would dart back and forth across the page, rarely taking in any information. Students beside me would seldom be reading (unless you were already a reader, and then this block was for you). One of my fondest memories is when my Grade 9 teacher would bring his book in and read. This provided ample opportunity for note writing (before the age of cell phones), and my friends and I would pass notes back and forth uninterrupted.

When I began my teaching career, I practiced what had been modeled for me: each day after lunch, we had silent reading. This block of time was one of my favorites as a new teacher. The students were quiet and I was encouraged to "model" reading myself by reading. Donalyn Miller, in her book *The Book Whisperer* (2009), urged teachers to model reading habits and practices with their students. I did this diligently (and it was an excellent opportunity for me to read during my day).

Over the next couple of years, I started noticing things about this block of time. Although I loved the quiet, it was evident that many students in my classroom were not reading. Additionally, 200 minutes a week for silent reading was cutting into my time with my students for other literacy activities. I knew reading for choice and pleasure was important, but I needed to figure out how to blend it into my schedule more flexibly.

As I played around with different ways of teaching literacy stations in my classroom, this station quickly became one of my favorites. Love to Read is simple: it allows students to read for pleasure. In my classroom and our Lit Pit, we created a cozy reading corner, our Love to Read spot. Students could read what they wanted, where they wanted, as long as it didn't disrupt others around them. The books I collected for my classroom library lived there. I often displayed books I wanted students to see as options and had various kinds of texts. Love to Read became my students' favorite station, an opportunity to "chill" and read something they had chosen.

I still believe in the importance of students seeing their teachers as readers. Reading rich mentor texts to my students, talking to them about what I am reading, and sharing book "commercials" for books they will enjoy are all opportunities to model lifelong reading to your students.

In the Classroom

Ms Kim's Grade 3 classroom is always abuzz. After morning recess, Ms Kim greets her students at the door. Behind her is a choice board of welcome options as they walk in. The choice board is a mixture of fun ways to say hello (*fist bump, mirror dance, smile, wave*) and literacy activities (*rhyme, syllables, spelling bee, same but different*). Students enter the classroom and choose one from each section. As Gavin enters, he chooses *mirror dance* and *same but different*. Ms Kim and Gavin give a little wiggle and a hop, and then Ms Kim says, "Tasty"; Gavin thinks for a while and replies excitedly, "Delicious!" Then he moves on into the classroom.

This morning's lesson is on checking for understanding. The Grade 3 class has been working hard at building stamina for the Love to Read station and are already at eleven minutes. Still, Ms Kim notices that sometimes students find it challenging to find something to talk to their partner about at the end of the station. Ms Kim talks about the importance of thinking while you read, and quickly gives examples of skills they have been learning in class. She then reads a quick story passage and asks students if they can summarize the key ideas. Ms Kim demonstrates the Five-Finger Retell and shows students how to check their understanding after they read quickly. She draws a giant hand on the board and shows how each finger can represent a question to ask themselves:

- Thumb: Character (Fiction), Topic (Nonfiction)
- Pointer Finger: Setting (Fiction), Main Idea (Nonfiction)

- Middle Finger: Main Problem or Conflict (Fiction), First Supporting Point (Nonfiction)
- Ring Finger: Key Events (Fiction), Second Supporting Point (Nonfiction)
- Baby Finger: How the Problem Is Resolved (Fiction), Third Supporting Point (Nonfiction)

Students practice as a whole group, doing the Five-Finger Retell with partners and then as an entire group. Later in the day, when students are reading information about local Indigenous plants, they practice the same Five-Finger Retell, using the new information they have read.

As Ms Kim sets up to start literacy stations, she reminds students of the expected behaviors and that they are working on building their reading stamina. Students check the board to find out which station they are at, and five students quickly head over to the Love to Read station. Before students start, Ms Kim comes to the Love to Read station and highlights some new books she has gathered. She reads a quick passage (that the students find hilarious) and says, "If you like books that make you laugh and enjoy reading about animals that act like humans, you should check out this book," then returns to her teacher station. Two students retrieve books from their bins, and three others find books off the shelves. Gavin quickly grabs the book that Ms Kim read from and gets right down to reading.

At the end of the station, Ms Kim allows students to share what they have read with each other. Two students share facts they learned in their books and ask questions of each other. Another group of three students find a page in one of the books, and all laugh as the one reader reads the dialogue in different voices. In the end, Ms Kim asks if anyone wants to share, and Gavin quickly shares (without spoiling) that the book he was reading was hilarious and even funnier than Ms Kim said. The next group of students coming to Love to Read excitedly ask if they can read that one next.

Ms Kim's classroom is full of stories and rich text. Everywhere you look, there are places and spaces for students to read; it is not uncommon to see students choosing to do so during choice time.

Whole-Class Instruction

Mentor Texts

Whole-class reading instruction is an excellent opportunity to introduce great mentor texts. Mentor texts are carefully selected pieces of writing that help students learn specific reading and writing skills. They provide examples of high-quality writing or reading comprehension skills that students can analyze, imitate, and apply to their work. Mentor texts can include books, poems, or any text that supports the skills you are trying to teach.

In reading instruction, mentor texts can be used to support students in various reading strategies. Mentor sentences written by the teacher can introduce students to new sounds or words they are learning. In the chapter Working with Words, we discuss decoding lessons; in Focus on Working with Text, we discuss rich lessons to help support students' comprehension. These whole-class lessons are deeply connected to the student's success in Love to Read.

Suggested Love to Read Lessons

- What Do Good Readers Do: Explicit teaching on the building blocks of reading habits and practices: strategies for choosing books, concepts of print, and building stamina and engagement.
- Reading Comprehension: Instruction on making meaning while you read; tied to Working with Text.
- When I Don't Know a Word: Explicit and systematic instruction on decoding strategies for students encountering a word they don't understand in Love to Read; tied to Working with Words.
- Talking About Books: Lessons on the importance of reflection and synthesizing the information we learn while we read and sharing it with others: Book Commercials (below), Did You Know? (page 71), Word Collectors (page 71).

Talking About Reading

Whole-class lessons that connect directly and explicitly to Love to Read involve students learning to talk about their reading. Richard Allington's research suggests that every reader should talk about what they read and write every day. A quick five minutes after literacy stations allows students to share what they have been reading and learning with their partners. Providing students with an opportunity to talk about what they read at the end of the station promotes rich oral language and encourages comprehension. Sharing their reading with a partner or a small group allows the students to highlight the information they have read and synthesize their understanding.

It is not enough to simply suggest that they turn and talk; you must give them instruction and practice on what and how to talk about their reading effectively. Students must have a book discussion modeled for them and have a place to practice before being released to try it independently. Often, when teachers share with me that these book talks become chatter in their classrooms, I discover that the students haven't learned how to talk about books effectively.

Book Commercials

Selling a great book to a partner or your class is one of my favorite parts of Love to Read stations. Early in the year, I share with the whole class to highlight new reading options in our classroom:

> *Do you love animals? Have you always wondered about how they feel? In this new book, we get an inside look at the thoughts and feelings of a gorilla trapped in a shopping mall zoo. If you love books about animals and aren't afraid to shed a few tears, and you wonder if a gorilla and a dog can be best friends. you will LOVE the book I just read,* The One and Only Ivan *by Katherine Applegate.*

As a lesson, students can watch commercials (the ones from the 1960s'-80s are real gems) and look at how the marketing team tried to sell their items. You can model a few great book commercials and then have students write their own. A vital aspect of this lesson is teaching students to highlight and tease but not spoil the critical elements of the book or text they are reading. Students can brainstorm ways to tempt their audience without giving too much of the book or text away. Students can write up some of their book commercials and share them outside the library or the classroom for other students to read.

Did You Know?

In this activity, students are encouraged to choose one or two key or main facts or ideas in the texts they are reading to share with a partner or group. Modeling this for your students is an excellent way of encouraging students to find key ideas or points of interest in their reading, and highlights the importance of knowing your audience, as well.

"Did you know that bees and dogs can smell fear?" is one of my favorite lines from the movie *Jerry Maguire*. The little boy in this 1996 classic endears himself into every movie watcher's heart as he offers Did You Know? facts to Tom Cruise's character. The movie clip reminds us of students' wide-eyed wonder at the world around them and their ability to retain interesting information. Asking students to look for Did You Know? facts in their reading provides a prompt and a reminder that great reading is about learning new things and collecting information. Even our youngest students can find interesting information from their reading. Highlighting the joy of new information and gathering these amazing facts gets students engaged and talking about their text.

If you have space as a class, you can collect Did You Know? facts on a bulletin board. Students can collect Did You Know? facts across all subject areas and in their reading at home.

Word Collectors

Peter H. Reynolds's book *The Word Collector* is a beautiful launch for another activity that can encourage students to talk about their reading. In the story, Jerome collects great words throughout his day. Read this book to your class (or any other books about great words) and encourage students to become word collectors.

Collecting words from their reading provides beautiful opportunities for students to add to their writing. Finding words in texts and encouraging students to use them in their written work highlights the importance of the reading–writing connection.

As students read, when they come across a word that they don't know, or that they just find interesting and exciting, they can "collect" that word. After you read the book, teach students what to do if they don't know the meaning of a word: look words up using a dictionary or a computer. Model how they can share their word and the definition with the class or a partner. Students can collect words throughout the year as individuals and as a class.

Building Stamina

Reading silently and on task for 20 minutes is a skill that needs to be taught, and even then might be an unrealistic expectation for some grades. Students might enter our classrooms having minimal reading modeled for them at home. Additionally, we are competing with a world of technology that has shortened students' attention spans. Reading habits and practices need to be modeled and practiced. Students need to see (and be taught) what readers do, and they need to build their reading muscles.

Reading *The Daily Five* by Gail Boushey and Joan Moser (2006) was transformative for teachers seeking to incorporate literacy stations into their classrooms. The book provided practical strategies for supporting students in literacy stations and emphasized the importance of building stamina. Modeling reading behaviors, creating anchor charts, and working together to build stamina became essential classroom practices.

During September and October, lessons focus on reading strategies, selecting enjoyable books, understanding what good readers do, thinking while reading, and discussing books through activities like book commercials. As a class, students collaboratively built stamina, gradually increasing the time spent engaged in reading. For many students, even in upper grades, independent reading is a skill that requires explicit teaching and practice—much like building muscles. Celebrating these successes fosters a positive and motivated classroom environment, as students grow in their reading stamina.

Although this practice can be tedious and feel like a chore, it is essential to building this framework in your classroom. Students must practice expected behaviors and work as a group to learn and practice the skills before you let them do it independently. Ideally, if your school adopts this practice as a whole, year after year, the students entering your classroom will already have practiced reading independently, and students will have to spend less time on building stamina.

Literacy Stations

Rich Text

Love to Read is a valuable space where students can explore any type of text they choose, with the only requirement being that they are actively reading. Comics, pamphlets, newspapers, and magazines can be great additions in your classroom library. This approach can face resistance from some who might question the value of allowing students to read "that garbage" during Love to Read. However, consistently emphasizing the station's purpose, encouraging students to love reading and make independent choices, helps shift perspectives over time. A strong rationale behind instructional choices not only guides practice but also equips you to address criticism and questions with confidence. It always comes back to knowing the purpose. Texts to include in Love to Read include

- Lists
- Letters
- Poems
- Texts attached to subjects you are studying
- Comics/Graphic Novels
- Magazines
- Pamphlets
- Stories (wide variety)
- Books of varying decodability, lengths, and instructional levels
- Student work

While running the Lit Pit, I encountered a student who was an extremely reluctant reader. He was a challenger and cared a lot about his social image. When I suggested he just hadn't met a book that he liked yet, he chose that as a challenge and immediately hated everything I showed him. The agreement in our Grade 5 classroom was that you had to give it a try and read at least 20 pages of a novel or the first third of a nonfiction pamphlet to decide. We had lessons on having an open mind and engaging with our reading. Yet, every time I would suggest a text, and he would "try" it and then gleefully tell me, "Nope, not for me." One day, in a discussion about things he liked to do on the weekends, he shared with me that he loved riding motorcycles with his dad. A lightbulb went off, and that day, I went and found every cool motorcycle magazine or how-to pamphlet I could find. This was a game changer—for him, motorcycle magazines were "cool" to read. They didn't hurt his social capital and he could flex his motorcycle knowledge with his pals. He had prior knowledge of bikes, which allowed him to decode better and comprehend the text he was reading, and he was interested. Motorcycles became my in and, eventually, we graduated to reading other materials. I even managed to convince him that he would love *The Mouse and the Motorcycle* the following year.

Rich and varied text is essential to a good Love to Read station. However, getting to know your students is also important. Early in your year with your students, part of the foundation of assessment is getting to know your students' interests and passions. These interests can provide you with tons of information about your students and texts they might be interested in. Likely, there will be students in your classrooms for whom you will have to work extra hard to introduce them to a book or text they like. However, this can also be a wonderful relationship-building time as you listen and learn your students' interests. Engaging your students in conversations about their interests and hobbies builds classroom culture and allows you to gain insight into the books you can introduce them to.

Instructional-Level Texts

Decodable texts can play an important part in literacy stations to support students decoding. These are the texts we use when we are reading with our students in Time with Teacher and in our practice of specific skills in Working with Words and Working with Text. But, although there is a critical time and place for just-right texts, Love to Read doesn't need to be that place.

For some teachers, flexibility for students to read for choice the whole time limits the time students can spend reading texts they can decode. In these cases, I suggest that teachers have students read one instructional, just-right text and the rest of the texts for choice (Allington, 2001; Gambrell, 2011; Reutzel & Cooter, 2005).

Students reading something they choose is an integral part of creating lifelong readers. Choosing texts they are interested in, even if the student isn't instructionally ready to read them independently, motivates them to learn to read. For many of our students who are emerging readers (particularly in some of the upper grades), reading time can be a visible indicator of their emerging skills. Early/decodable readers (especially decodable) are often of low interest and are often developmentally behind the age of the readers, who need to use them to practice.

Love to Read is an opportunity to instill the love of reading (and the motivation to do so). For my student who I referenced above, his ability (and freedom) to read motorcycle magazines motivated him to want to learn some of the reading strategies to help him decode and comprehend those magazines. It opened the door to the importance of reading. If he had been allowed to read only texts at his reading level, this *aha!* moment wouldn't have happened.

Add novelty to reading:
- Flashlight Reading: reading by flashlight
- Fireplace Vibes: put on the fireplace channel, so students can read by the fire
- Read to a Stuffy: students bring in their favorite stuffy to read with
- Nature Reading: have the Love to Read group (or all your literacy stations) outside for a day
- Buddy Read: read to a friend or younger or older buddy

Teacher Tweaks

For teachers who have silent reading in their timetable, adding Love to Read to your literacy stations frees up significant time in your day. There might still be times in your classroom when you choose to have the whole class participate in silent reading; however, this can be a strategy designed to support students' social-emotional learning and provide students with time to regulate, instead of daily, whole-class silent reading practice.

Reflection is an essential part of effective teaching and learning. At the end of chapters 3 to 7, you have opportunities to reflect on what you've read, your practice, and ways to move forward. Tweak, Toss, Treasure is a reflective practice for teachers, and it works great for kids as well.

Learning from My Mistakes

Over the years in my teaching career, and in modeling its use with other teachers, I have made many mistakes in my Love to Read station. Early on, I set up a great spot for students to read but failed to model the expectations of what effective reading looked like. In my first few years, I noticed the reading behaviors slipping and realized that the time spent actually reading was quickly dissolving. I ignored students' behaviors as long as they did not disrupt those around them. At the end of the station, students would put away their books and quickly move to the next station without an opportunity to discuss what they were reading.

As this station and my learning have developed, I learned the importance of modeling, modeling, and modeling. Even though it may feel monotonous, co-creating expectations for what good readers do and building the stamina to read for extended periods is a critical component of this station running smoothly. Additionally, students must be redirected to the expected behaviors when the reading stops. Consistency and clarity are the keys to a successful literacy station routine.

Another critical error was not letting students discuss what they had read. Allowing students to share their learning gave them intention and purpose, ensuring they were using reading time effectively. Knowing they would have to talk about their reading at the end of each station motivated many students to read with purpose. Additionally, the possibility of sharing book commercials, cool facts through Did You Know?, and vocabulary in their word collections provided students with intentionality. (Providing students with options for what to discuss after they are done reading does not mean they must share all three.)

Modeling different ways to talk about text gives students many choices in things they could share, but without the pressure to share everything. Another critical mistake is asking students to do too much after reading, taking the joy from the reading. The key is finding a balance between providing an opportunity to talk about what they have read and being able to read for the joy of reading. This balance takes some practice and often depends on the students in your class.

Another mistake I made, and maybe the most critical, is not remembering the point to this station—instilling in students a love of reading so that they can find meaning and engagement in reading, ideally instilling in them a desire to continue to grow as readers (and choose it as a lifelong habit).

Tweak/Toss/Treasure

Tweak

- What is something you are currently doing to support your students' love of reading that you could tweak slightly? Are there opportunities in your classroom for students to read something they choose?

Toss

- What is something that you are currently doing in your classroom as a way for students to practice their reading that is no longer serving your purpose? What activities or practices are you currently doing that do not have the outcome you hoped? Do they need to be let go?

Treasure

- What is a takeaway from this chapter that you can easily integrate into your classroom practice? How does your teaching practice help support students to learn to love reading?

6

Writing

> "A word after a word after a word is power."
> — Margaret Atwood

> "You should write because you love the shape of stories and sentences and the creation of different words on a page. Writing comes from reading, and reading is the finest teacher of how to write."
> — Annie Proulx

Writing instruction doesn't have to be something teachers and students dread. Learning to write, and having the opportunity to do so, empowers students to communicate their ideas and craft meaningful stories from their imaginations and experiences. This chapter explores strategies for combining reading and writing instruction, along with structured lessons to inspire students to write. You'll also discover how to set up an engaging and effective writing station that fosters creativity and helps students grow as confident, skilled writers.

The purpose of writing instruction is to inspire students to learn and, ideally, enjoy the writing process. The lessons in this chapter provide explicit instruction and meaningful opportunities for students to practice and develop their writing abilities. Love to Write is a literacy station where students engage in self-chosen writing tasks while focusing on the skills they need to advance their writing.

During my school career, I had developed the belief that I was not a writer and was often reminded of my terrible spelling. I always knew I had good ideas; I just wasn't sure how to effectively get them onto paper. The thought of teaching students to write, and possibly even learn to enjoy it, felt like a monumental task and a terrifying prospect.

Writing is easier to teach with a plan. Many students are reluctant to write for many reasons, and motivating them to practice independently can be incredibly frustrating. Writing lessons often focus more on the writing product than the writing process. For example, one of my favorite lessons is based on the book *The Best Part of Me* by Wendy Ewald. As a whole class, we would read this excellent book, and students would write, following the examples of the writing in the book. Although this was a great mentor text, I missed the opportunity to teach a writing skill during the process. I was focused on the product of the writing rather than using the mentor texts as a guide for the qualities of effective writing.

Often my writing instruction involved writing activities, and was not guided by the skills I wanted the students to learn. Activity after activity, the students would write, yet there was not necessarily any growth in the students' writing.

When I started integrating Four Blocks Literacy (Cunningham & Hall, 1998) into my classroom, the writing block provided more explicit instruction in teaching writing skills. This shift in approach transformed how I planned my writing lessons. I began seeking ways to offer students opportunities to create personally meaningful work while developing the skills necessary to improve their writing abilities.

Writing instruction, like reading instruction, demands intentional and systematic teaching of skills. It also needs to be explicitly taught. The more I have researched, the more I see how reading and writing are linked. Students who are taught strategies to decode words using different skills can use those same strategies to encode words in their writing.

Love to Write was born from Richard Allington's research in *Every Child, Every Day* (2012). He outlined that every student should write something personally meaningful daily and talk about their writing with their peers. Love to Write allows our students to write freely and for joy.

In my classroom, I identified essential writing skills that required explicit instruction and continued using mentor texts to teach and inspire my students. I explicitly taught these skills during whole-class instruction, added them to the classroom Editor's Checklist, and integrated them as expectations for all student writing. However, I was still struggling to find time in my schedule for students to practice these writing skills, so I began looking for opportunities for students to practice their writing skills during literacy station activities.

In the Classroom

Ms Manning's Grade 6 classroom is buzzing with the low hum of quiet conversation. When you enter her classroom, you notice groups of students working in different areas around the room. On the wall, there is a large whiteboard with an Editor's Checklist depicted. There are many learning targets listed under headings (Organization, Meaning, Voice, and Conventions), and one student appears to be using it as an anchor chart to check his work. Students are scattered around the room, busily writing. Sam is writing while lying on his stomach on the floor. His page is covered in small squares with pictures in each, capturing a fabulous story about Dexter Mallow, a marshmallow man. He shares the ongoing story he is creating and how he continues it each time he is at Love to Write. Alexis sits at a desk. Her page is filled with an organizational web of information about horses and riding. She explains that horses are a newfound interest and she has been doing some research (trying to convince her parents to let her start horseback riding). Her web is in the beginning stages, and she is working to organize her thinking before creating her persuasive writing for her parents. Greyson types with a computer on his lap, revising a piece of writing he has already done. He looks up and down at the Editor's Checklist in front of him as he makes edits to his work. He shares that Ms Manning read his work over in his Time with Teacher yesterday and gave him some feedback on things to improve.

At the end of station time, when the chime rings, the students at Love to Write pair up and share their writing. The students give constructive feedback and ask questions about the purpose and audience of their writing. After a few minutes, Ms Manning asks the whole class if anyone would like to share their learning, and Sam enthusiastically shares a few key moments from his next installment of his Dexter Mallow comic. Ms Manning suggests that if he chooses to take it to a published copy, it would have a welcome place in their Love to Read library.

Across the hall in the Grade 2 classroom, Mr Mac sits with his students on the carpet. On the whiteboard behind him is the learning target: *I can write a story with a clear beginning, middle, and end that organizes my ideas.* He is rereading aloud the story *One Day, The End* by Rebecca Kai Dotlich and Fred Koehler. He stops at each page, and students turn and discuss with their partners all the things happening on the page that the illustrator drew but the author didn't write about. Mr Mac uses this book as a mentor text to discuss the beginning, middle, and end, and the organization of writing. They take one page from the story and look at the pictures and the words. They put ideas in the three columns that Mr Mac has drawn on the whiteboard (Beginning, Middle, and End).

The students move from the floor into different desk groupings around the classroom. Each group has a whiteboard and a copied page from the book. The groups discuss what the pictures tell about what is happening in the beginning, middle, and end, and record it on their whiteboard in the three columns they have drawn. Mr. Mac walks around to each group, asking guiding questions and giving feedback. After a few minutes, he brings them all back to the carpet to recap. They share their learning, and the class ends with a quick recap of the lesson target and a reminder of the importance of clearly organizing your ideas. Mr Mac explains that students will have an opportunity to practice finding the beginning, middle, and end in their Working with Text station later today and that they can use this to organize their writing at Love to Write, with the prompt, One Day I ________.

As students move to their literacy stations, the Love to Write group sits down and begins. Damon takes out a small notebook and begins writing in his "text" book (see page 89). He passed his book to his big buddy earlier in the week and is excited to read what his buddy responded. He works quickly to read and answer the questions and follows up with a few more questions. Gabby works on a story she began in class. Her personal writing goal focuses on adding more detail to her writing, and she diligently adds descriptive details to her story. Jordan is a student working well above grade level in writing and reading, who often looks for opportunities to extend their learning. Jordan loves to write and has been working on a sloth research paper. They are adding text features to their writing and making edits from the feedback they received from their Time with Teacher station yesterday. At the end of the station, the students share their work with each other, and give feedback on something they loved and could add next time.

Whole-Class Instruction

Mentor Texts

We can use the same mentor text for whole-class instruction of both reading and writing. After we have looked at the text as an example of a reading strategy (decoding or comprehension), we can take another look at it through the lens of *What did the author do?* Looking at texts through an author's lens allows students to see high-quality examples of sentence structure, word choice, organization, ideas, and voice. Using a variety of mentor texts also provides students with examples of writers' purpose and audience and serves as an example for different writing forms.

Mentor texts

- Provide purpose: Real-world examples of rich text provide students with examples that inspire their reading and writing (Gallagher, 2011).
- Model explicit skills: bridging the gap between reading and writing processes (Graves, 2003).
- Stretch student thinking: Instructional strategies that are just beyond students' instructional level allow students to see strategies in action before trying them themselves (Vygotsky, 1978).
- Support the reading–writing connection: reading with a writer's lens and analyzing why authors make specific choices (Gallagher, 2011).

Using a mentor text to teach reading and writing strategies is an excellent way to connect the two.

Reading Skill	**Writing Skill**	**Mentor Text Examples**
Sequence: Identifying the order and sequence of texts (what happened in the beginning, middle, and end)	Sequence: Organizing your ideas into beginning, middle, and end. Use transitional words *first*, *next*, *then*, and *finally* to tell or retell a story.	*The Very Hungry Caterpillar* by Eric Carle *The Snowy Day* by Ezra Jack Keats
Repetition: Notice author's use of repetition for emphasis in a story	Repetition: Creating a simple pattern in your writing	*Brown Bear, Brown Bear, What Do You See?* by Bill Martin Jr. *If You Give a Mouse a Cookie* by Laura Numeroff
Visualizing: What words help create pictures while you read	Word Choice: What words can you choose that help create vivid descriptions for your reader?	*The Gruffalo* by Julia Donaldson *The Black Book of Colors* by Menena Cottin
Finding the Main Idea and Supporting Points	Crafting a main idea and supporting points	*Owl Moon* by Jane Yolen *All Are Welcome* by Alexandra Penfold
Making Connections (to the text)	Using personal connections to add depth to writing	*The Recess Queen* by Alexis O'Neill *The Man with the Violin* by Kathy Stinson & Dušan Petričić
Inference: Using context clues to infer meaning	Show, Don't Tell writing: Use language that allows the reader to infer, not be explicitly told	*Alexander and the Terrible, No Good, Very Bad Day* by Judith Viorst *The Sweetest Fig* by Chris Van Allsburg

Author Purpose: Identifying why the author wrote the text	Identifying your purpose and choosing an appropriate style to convey meaning	*One Plastic Bag* by Miranda Paul *Can I Be Your Dog?* by Troy Cummings *What If You Had Animal Teeth?* by Sandra Markle
Perspective: Determining the narrator's or character's perspective	Perspective Writing: Writing from a consistent point of view and experimenting with different perspectives	*They All Saw a Cat* by Brendan Wetzel *The True Story of the Three Little Pigs* by Jon Scieszka *Voices in the Park* by Anthony Browne *I Am the Dog, I Am the Cat* by Donald Hall
Vocabulary: Decoding the meaning of vocabulary based on context	Vocabulary: Using rich and varied vocabulary to add depth to writing	*The Gruffalo* by Julia Donaldson *The Word Collector* by Peter H. Reynolds *The Lotus Seed* by Sherry Garland *Stacey's Extraordinary Words* by Stacey Abrams
Summarizing: Condensing text into its main idea and key points	Organizing your writing into main idea and key points, and using that as a guide for writing	*The Important Book* by Margaret Wise Brown *How to Write a Story* by Kate Messner *Martin's Big Words* by Doreen Rappaport
Character: Understanding character traits, motivations, and developments	Character: Creating main characters with clear traits and motivations	*Enemy Pie* by Derek Munson *The Invisible Boy* by Patrice Barton
Recognizing Text Features: Using headings, subheadings, tables, etc., to help understand the text	Text Features: Using text features, headings, subheadings, etc., to help support writing	*Your Fantastic Elastic Brain* by JoAnn Deak *A Seed Is Sleepy* by Dianna Hutts Aston
Figurative Language: Recognizing author's use of literary elements to help support writing and add depth	Figurative Language: Using literary elements in writing to engage readers	*Fireflies!* by Julie Brinckloe *My Mouth Is a Volcano* by Julia Cook *My Dog Is As Smelly As Dirty Socks* by Hanoch Piven

Editor's Checklist

Students benefit from a visual reminder of the skills they have learned in whole-class instructions. One of the most effective ways to do this is through an Editor's Checklist, a tool that provides students with a visual cue of the skills and writing characteristics they need to include in their written work. As a whole-class lesson is taught in writing, and students have had time to practice it, it is added to the class's anchor chart. These skills become no-excuse skills and are expected in the student's written work.

As I tend to have a flair for the dramatic in my teaching, I told my students that I would throw dramatic temper tantrums if I found these "mistakes" in their writing. This works, until you encounter a student who wants to test your resolve and intentionally leaves all the ending punctuation out of their writing. After my dramatic temper tantrum, I changed my threat to something less tempting for students. However, the message remained the same: once we learn it, we apply it to all aspects of our writing. This visual reminder of whole-class writing expectations also demonstrates that the learning is meaningful, valuable, and necessary. Students know that when it goes up on our Editor's Checklist, it is a big deal, and that we are growing in our expectations of our students as writers.

Students can use the Editor's Checklist to review their writing and look for evidence of their individual writing goals when reviewing and refining it.

Individual Editor's Checklists are also excellent ways of working on students' personal writing goals. As a whole class, you might be working on a scope of writing skills, but individual writing goals for students provide goals that either extend their skills beyond the class expectations or support writing skills they might not have yet mastered from previous grades.

Meeting the Needs of All Learners

Students enter our classroom with varying abilities and levels of engagement in different subject areas. This is particularly true in writing. Year after year, my students varied enormously in their interest in writing and their writing ability. The lack of engagement, paired with emerging skills, made writing instruction challenging to plan and practice, as often students had a wide range of abilities. Managing the wide range of student needs is challenging in every subject area. It frequently involves planning multiple iterations of the same lesson to ensure that all needs are met. This can be both daunting and time-consuming.

Targeted whole-class lessons focused on specific skills, often guided by a scope and sequence and connected to rich mentor texts, provide an easy way to differentiate instruction. Low Floor, High Ceiling writing activities let students engage with the task at their skill level, encouraging growth and creativity.

Teacher Tip
Have students underline the evidence of their goal in green in their writing. For instance, if a student is working on varying their sentences to add interest for the reader, they can underline different sentence starters in their writing to draw attention to how they are implementing that goal into their writing.

Individual writing goals are also effective ways of providing personal support to the students' writing process. As students engage in lessons that teach them effective ways of giving descriptive feedback and have a class Editor's Checklist that they can use to support their writing and editing process, they can also begin to look for ways to grow in their writing. During Time with Teacher, you can support your students in looking at their writing and coming up with individualized writing goals. Our students write their writing goals on a chart in their writing folders. Quick check-ins with students about their writing goals (during Time with Teacher) allows you to differentiate writing instruction based on their needs.

Whole-Class Lessons

When trying to determine which skills your students need to learn, begin with (if you have them) the skills determined by your school or district's curriculum. Next, look at what skills your individual students, and whole class, need to further their writing instruction. Teaching writing is complex, as writing instruction is not a linear process. Joan Sedita's Writing Rope (2023) illustrates the complexity and interconnectedness of writing skills. Sedita illustrates the strands of Critical Thinking, Syntax, Text Structure, Transcription, and Writing Craft weaving into skilled writing. Similarly, 6 plus 1 Writing Traits (Culham, 2018) organizes its writing skills into Ideas, Organization, Word Choice, Voice, Sentence Fluency, Conventions, and Presentation. Looking to these resources for ways to organize your writing instruction can provide guidance, both research-based and teacher-friendly, in ways to organize your whole-class writing lessons.

Writing and reading instruction works best when connected rather than taught separately. Studies suggest that effective reading and writing are interconnected and reinforce one another. When students engage in comprehension activities that examine structure, word choice, and voice, they can recognize the techniques and begin examining strategies for applying them in their writing.

Mentor texts offer students valuable opportunities to analyze a piece of text, first as readers and then as writers. This dual perspective deepens their understanding of reading and writing, encouraging them to think critically and creatively about an author's choices and apply those techniques to their work. See chart on page 78.

Read it Like a Reader, Read it like a Writer, then Write

For much of my career, I taught reading and writing as separate subjects, with dedicated blocks for each every day. That changed when I realized the power of connecting the two. By integrating reading and writing, I gained valuable time in my schedule and created a more cohesive learning experience.

This shift also transformed my students' attitudes toward writing. Many had labeled themselves "not a writer" or dismissed their ideas because they weren't "good spellers." Writing felt like a chore for many, and their reluctance became a challenge I was determined to address. By linking reading and writing, I saw a positive shift in how my students engaged with both. Using rich mentor texts and teaching the reading–writing connection helped minimize the reluctance of many of my students to write. When students immerse themselves in a great story and start analyzing the author's choices, they often forget they're discussing writing techniques.

Modeled Writing

As back in my school days, when the teacher would write on the overhead projector (I know I'm aging myself), students benefit from watching proficient writers write, from seeing our writing process as teachers continue to model the ongoing refining nature of writing. Modeling the writing-and-refining process allows students to see their writing as a work in progress. Using a document camera or chart paper, or projecting off your computer, writing in front of your students and talking them through your thinking process can be a rich learning opportunity for students.

Using student exemplars can also be an effective way of modeling writing with your students. Past students' work can provide opportunities for students to work together to provide descriptive feedback and highlight compelling writing pieces. Discussing the author's choices (and seeing peers as authors) prompts students to think critically about their decisions in their writing.

Ralph Tells a Story by Abby Hanlon is an excellent book with many lesson opportunities; e.g., ideas, oral storytelling. In one lesson, I write pieces of Ralph's writing, telling students I found them in my classroom. The students use Ralph's writing as a practice for giving feedback, and we look for ways to support Ralph in moving his writing forward. I explain to students that they should put their "editor's hat on" and give Ralph feedback on what he was doing well and what areas for growth he had. For younger students, you can use strategies like Two Stars and a Wish or Great and Growth. I intentionally scaffold Ralph's writing samples to show improvement and tie them to lessons we will work on in class. Students are keen to give Ralph feedback on his writing and love commenting on how much his writing has improved since his writing in the book.

One of my favorite activities with Kindergarten and Grade 1 students (although I have used this lesson with students all the way to Grade 5) involves using a character's writing to help launch the Editor's Checklist and model giving descriptive feedback.

Whether it's modeled writing by you as the teacher, by other students, or even by imaginary characters, the goal remains the same: engaging students in observing the writing process in action. Students gain valuable insights by watching the thinking and writing process unfold and exploring ways to provide feedback to refine and edit the work.

Practical Tips for Modeling Writing

- Be intentional: Focus on specific skills you want to highlight (generating ideas, hooking your reader, transition words, varying sentences, editing for clarity).
- Engage students in the process: Ask students questions and let them add ideas through the process (*How would you make this sentence more interesting?*).
- Show real struggles: Consider your students' challenges and model them in the modeled writing, showing ways to overcome those challenges (finding the right word, not knowing how to spell something, writer's block).

- Revise and revisit: Use student texts as opportunities to revise and revisit as mentor texts in future lessons or station activities (Working with Words: Use writing as a mentor text, and students find other words that say the same things; Love to Write: Students can edit and revise the writing or use it as a model for their writing).

Suggested Writing Lessons

Kindergarten and Grade 1

This list is not exhaustive, but designed to indicate basic writing skills.

Ideas
- I can identify different types of writing (letters, stories, nonfiction).
- I can brainstorm ideas for my story.
- I can tell about a topic, with a few facts.
- I can begin to connect ideas to a topic.

Organization
- I can tell a story.
- I can retell a story (beginning, middle, and end).
- I can label and draw pictures to tell a story.
- I can use items to tell (or retell) a story.
- I can retell a story in my own words, in order.
- I can draw a picture (informational) and write a sentence.

Word Choice
- I can identify different words to use to describe a picture or an item.
- I can choose words to describe what I want to say.
- I can identify words in a story that help the author state their point.

Sentence Fluency
- I can model sentence writing, using a sentence stem.
- I can begin to write simple sentences.

Voice
- I can identify words the author chooses to add personality to their writing.
- I can identify words the author uses to express emotion.
- I can identify words I can use to express emotions.

Conventions
- I can use finger spaces.
- I can use words I know to create stories.
- I can identify ending punctuation.
- I can begin to use ending punctuation.
- I can begin to use capitals at the beginning of my sentences.
- I can begin to use capitals for important people and places.
- I can capitalize *I* in my writing.
- I can begin to use phonetic patterns to spell words correctly.
- I can correctly use high-frequency words that I have learned in my writing.

Grades 2 and 3

Ideas
- I can generate ideas for my writing.
- I can write about a topic with supporting facts and details.
- I can gather information about a topic and plan my writing.

- I can add details to support my main idea.
- I can identify purposes and audiences for my writing.

Organization
- I can organize my ideas into a beginning, middle, and end.
- I can organize my ideas into a topic sentence and supporting details.
- I can use a variety of graphic organizers to organize my ideas.
- I can plan my writing.
- I can use a plan to organize my writing.
- I can organize my ideas into a paragraph.

Sentence Fluency
- I can write simple sentences.
- I can write compound sentences.
- I can use a variety of sentences to add to my writing.
- I can introduce my topic with a topic sentence that captivates the reader.
- I can group related information together in my writing.
- I can conclude my writing effectively.
- I can start my sentences in a variety of ways.

Voice
- I can identify ways to add personality to my writing.
- I can add words that express emotion in my writing.
- I can use language to convey my meaning.

Word Choice
- I can use adjectives to add to my writing.
- I can identify words that add variety to my writing.
- I can add words to my writing that help the reader visualize.
- I can use a variety of words to my writing to add interest.

Conventions
- I can use capital letters appropriately in my writing.
- I can use commas in my writing.
- I can begin to use quotation marks.
- I can begin to use apostrophes appropriately.
- I can vary my ending punctuation appropriately.
- I can use a variety of phonemic patterns to spell words correctly.
- I can spell a variety of high-frequency words consistently in my writing.

Grades 4 and 5

Ideas
- I can identify the purpose of my writing and choose the format appropriately.
- I can identify different audiences and plan my writing accordingly.
- I can write effectively about a topic using supporting details.
- I can gather information about a topic and plan my writing.
- I can add details to support my main idea.
- I can plan, write, and edit my writing.

Organization
- I can organize my thoughts using a variety of organizers.
- I can organize my writing into a clear beginning, middle, and end.
- I can organize my ideas into topic sentences, paragraphs, and clear conclusions.

- I can use transition words and phrases to link my ideas, sentences, and/or paragraphs.
- I can write an engaging topic sentence to hook my readers.
- I can write for a variety of purposes and audiences.

Sentence Fluency
- I can write compound sentences.
- I can write a variety of sentences to add variety and interest to my writing.
- I can identify run-on and incomplete sentences.
- I can write ending sentences or conclusions to effectively sum up my writing.

Voice
- I can write from a specific point of view.
- I can add personality to my writing.
- I can develop a reader's interest through the way that I write.

Word Choice
- I can use strong word choice to add interest to my writing.
- I can use language to convey my meaning.
- I can use some literary devices to add impact to my writing.
- I can add words to my writing that help the reader visualize.
- I can use a variety of words to my writing to add interest.
- I can take risks with complex words and vocabulary.

Conventions
- I am beginning to use present, future, and past tense appropriately.
- I can use capital letters appropriately in my writing.
- I can use commas in my writing.
- I can use quotation marks.
- I can use apostrophes appropriately.
- I can vary my ending punctuation.
- I can use a variety of phonemic patterns to spell words correctly.
- I can spell a variety of high-frequency words consistently in my writing.

Sample Love to Write Lesson

Point	Learning Targets Reading: I can identify the key elements of an argument in a piece of writing. Writing: I can support my opinion with reasons and key details.
Product	*Hey, Little Ant* by Hannah and Phillip Hoose is an excellent resource for teaching both persuasive writing and perspective-taking.
Process	Activate • Read Aloud and Present the Problem: Read aloud *Hey, Little Ant* to students. Afterward, present the central question: "Should the boy step on the ant?" Acquire Group Activity: Take a Side • Split students into small groups. Assign each group the perspective of the *Ant* or the *Boy*.

	• In their groups, students will
	    • Use ideas from the text to identify reasons supporting their assigned side.
	    • Work together to develop key arguments for why the boy should step on the ant (*Boy* group) or why the ant should go free (*Ant* group).
	
	Partner Debate
	• Pair each student with someone from the opposing side (one *Ant* student and one *Boy* student).
	• Have them take turns presenting their arguments to one another.
	
	Whole-Class Discussion
	• Reconvene as a class and create a chart that lists reasons from both sides on the board.
	• Include any additional evidence that students come up with beyond the text.
	• Guide students in analyzing the chart, identifying which reasons are the strongest and why.
	• Ask students to share what makes a piece of evidence effective.
	• Conclude by voting on which side presented the most compelling evidence.

People (UDL)	Emerging Learners: Students who need additional support can use speech-to-text for their persuasive writing, or can work alongside a peer or adult to organize their writing and list key words ahead of time. Extending Learners: To extend the writing, students can research additional information that goes beyond the story to help support their position. Students who are going beyond the learning might need additional instruction on the difference between evidence and opinion to help persuade their audience in their writing.

Practice (Whole Class)	Apply
	Independent Writing: Persuasive Paragraph
	• Have students consider their personal opinion: *Should the boy step on the ant or let him go free?*
	• Students write a persuasive paragraph (or a few sentences) supporting their opinion with evidence from the story.
	• Teach the structure of a strong persuasive paragraph:
	    • State your opinion.
	    • Provide a rationale to support your opinion using strong evidence.
	    • Conclude by restating your opinion.

Practice (Literacy Station)	Students can write other persuasive pieces using the same guidelines in the Love to Write station. If you have space near your writing station, you can place prompts for students looking for ideas on what to write about; e.g., *Should recess be longer? What is the best pet? Should technology be allowed in schools? What is the best season?* In Working with Text, students can look at various texts and determine their opinions and supporting points.

Add On	Students could use *Hey, Little Ant* as an example text and write two different sides of a debate (from two different perspectives). They could write individually or work with a partner to write from separate perspectives on an issue. For instance, writing from a person's perspective and a pet's perspective on whether or not you should take your pet for a walk. Or writing from a teacher's perspective and a student's perspective on whether or not candy should be allowed as a snack (or cell phones in schools).

Literacy Station

Providing visual prompts for students supports their writing. If space is at a premium in your classroom, tri-fold boards can be an excellent way to display information for the students' writing section. These tri-folds can be placed anywhere in the room and brought out only when necessary.

Over the years, I have experimented with many ways of organizing Love to Write. It often comes down to the space available in your classroom and how you like to use it. Ideally, in the younger years, students would have access to alphabet charts, idea prompts, high-frequency word lists, and an Editor's Checklist. Some teachers also choose to have sound walls as visual references for their students.

A writing folder is my favorite tool for organizing student writing. The setup can vary depending on your writing program, but I recommend folders with pockets to store student work. Include a prompt sheet at the front with writing ideas (many teachers use Adrienne Gear's *Brain Pockets* activity from her book *Writing Power*, 2011) and a section at the back for individual writing goals or a personalized Editor's Checklist. These folders fit easily into students' literacy bags—large freezer bags work great—alongside instructional-level texts and station activities for portability.

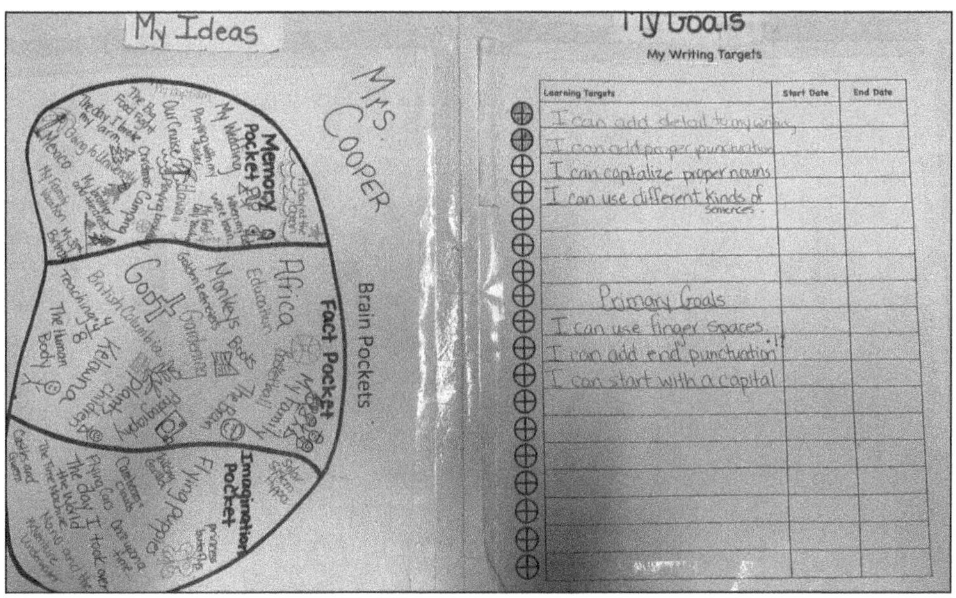

It might seem ironic that a book outlining a framework for literacy development discusses another possible framework. However, in my experience, many teachers choose to use their beloved Writers Workshop framework inside literacy stations, where it works seamlessly.

Writers Practice

A writing workshop is a flexible framework for teaching writing that emphasizes frequent, meaningful writing opportunities, explicit instruction, and ongoing feedback. Originally shaped by educators like Donald Graves (*Writing: Teachers and Children at Work*, 1983) and Lucy Calkins (*The Art of Teaching Writing*,

1986), the model was built on the belief that students grow as writers through regular practice, voice and choice, and authentic purpose. At its core, writing workshop values student voice, agency, and the continuous nature of the writing process; drafting, revising, editing, and publishing.

Many of the structural elements of Writers Workshop, such as dedicated time to write, focused mini-lessons, conferring, and opportunities to reflect and share are relevant today. Particularly when paired with explicit, systematic instruction in writing organization, structure, voice, sentence fluency, and conventions.

The writing workshop structure allows teachers to balance whole class instruction with independent practice and responsive, small-group or individual feedback. When aligned with current research informed practices, including modeling, guided practice, and clearly defined success criteria, writing workshop can be a powerful tool in a comprehensive literacy program.

In this framework, Love to Write becomes the time when students apply what they've learned through independent writing, while Time with Teacher serves as an opportunity for targeted feedback, instruction, or guided practice. The routine offers predictability, practice, and the opportunity for growth over time. Individual (on their writing folders) and whole-class writing goals (Editor's checklist) can provide supportive structures to help students continue to grow in their writing skills.

Writers Workshop Format

- Targeted Lesson and explicit instruction: Whole-class lesson
- Student Writing Time: during Love to Write
- Conferring: during Time with Teacher
- Sharing: at the end of station time

Activities

Your choice of activities at your Love to Write station depends on how you focus this station; this can change year after year, depending on your students. Love to Write can be run similarly to Love to Read, where students practice writing for joy. It can be open-ended, with students writing whatever they want, and where prompts are present for those struggling to find ideas. Love to Write can also be an extension of the Writers Workshop that you run in your classroom, where students use the Love to Write station as a student writing opportunity. Students who prefer a more structured writing approach can practice the writing activities you have taught in your lessons. Some teachers prefer a structured writing station where students have activities to complete. In these situations, I suggest that you give students an opportunity to have some voice and choice in what they write about.

Lists, Letters, and More

Writing can take various forms and formats. In the early primary years, the Love to Write station can consist of students' storytelling using loose parts, puppets, or other items. Oral storytelling can grow to include drawing pictures, labeling, and other forms of writing. Students can engage in storytelling using materials to help support their storytelling. Lessons teaching students the beginning, middle, and end can support students in organizing both storytelling and story writing.

For reluctant writers, providing less daunting forms of writing can often be a gateway into the writing process. Providing students with prompts for list writing (e.g., write a list of all your favorite people, a list of all the foods you love, a list of what you're grateful for) can be an easy entry point for emergent writers. Letter writing is also an excellent way of engaging students in the writing process.

"Text" Books

One of my favorite ways to get my oldest daughter to write in her primary years was through our "text" book. Since we didn't allow her cell phones at a young age, Lexy and I created this alternative: she would "text" me by writing a message and a few questions in a notebook. then leave it under my pillow at night. I'd "text" her back and return it under her pillow. This simple activity encouraged her to write, and the book became a treasured keepsake for me, even 20 years later.

Copy this

Dear ______,

"Message Me" — a special notebook where I write messages to you, and you write back!

How it works:

1. I'll write you a note, question, or message.
2. You read it and write back in this book.
3. We keep the conversation going—just like texting, but on paper!
4. **If I make a mistake in my spelling or grammar, that's okay!** You can kindly model the correct spelling or sentence in your message back to me. Writing back and forth helps me build confidence, grow as a reader and writer, and discover the joy of written conversations!

Let's have fun, share stories, ask questions, and write back and forth!

This idea works beautifully in the classroom, too. Students can "text" their teacher, other adults in the school, classmates, or buddies as part of a Love to Write activity, fostering creativity and written communication skills. These little notebooks can also be great to send home to families to practice writing at home. It is important to let parents know the purpose (to get students writing) and remind them not to correct the students' spelling or grammar but to model it back to their children. A note home to parents with the book can provide examples of how to model writing to their children and prompt them with ways to ask good questions their kids can respond to.

SI (Student Intelligence): An Idea for Upper Grades

With the introduction of artificial intelligence, the conversation about how it affects student writing and learning has taken centre stage. Wherever possible, I look for ways to engage students in areas and topics they are already familiar with and interested in. Student Intelligence (SI) is a play on Artificial Intelligence: in this activity, students take a simple sentence and, like AI, find different ways to say the same thing. They can provide multiple options for the same sentence and then vote on which response they like best. As a lesson to introduce this activity, you can show students how an AI platform can take your sentence and rewrite it for clarity or interest. The students can vote on their favorites and then do the same. This effectively demonstrates to students that there are many different ways to say the same thing and highlights that some are more effective than others.

Sentence: I went to the park to play with my friends.

CHATGPT Response:

- I visited the park, and I played games with my friends there.
- When I arrived at the park, I joined my friends to play.
- I headed to the playground to hang out and have fun with my buddies.
- I strolled to the vibrant park to enjoy some games with my lively friends.

Possible Student Response

- I went to the neighborhood park to play with my friends Megan and Marty.
- My friends and I went to the park.
- The park is a great place to go to play with my friends.

Reflecting on Their Writing

See page 92 for a template for student Writing Self-Assessment.

Students gain a great deal from discussing their writing with peers. Whether between station rotations or at the end of literacy stations, just five minutes for students to share their work with a classmate is time well spent. While this process requires teaching and modeling expectations, once students understand the routine, it transforms into a meaningful and enriching part of their learning experience.

During this time, students can share a sentence or two they are proud of, or a piece of their writing that they revised. Giving students time to talk also allows them to be accountable for using their time effectively during Love to Write. As a teacher, I can use this time to check in with my more reluctant students to check their understanding and clarify any skills that need improvement. Consider supplying Writing Talks sentence starters:

I'm proud of ____________.
I changed this ______________ because ___________.
What do you think about ________?
My writing goal is ___________, and I showed evidence of it here: ____________.
Next time in Love to Write, I'm hoping to ____________.

At the end of the literacy station time, students can share their learning from any station. Often, students will choose to share what they wrote about, providing a wonderful opportunity for students to learn from one another.

Reflection is an essential part of effective teaching and learning. At the end of chapters 3 to 7, you have opportunities to reflect on what you've read, your practice, and ways to move forward. Tweak, Toss, Treasure is a reflective practice for teachers, and it works great for kids as well.

Teacher Tweaks

Finding time in class schedules for students to practice writing or write for pleasure can be challenging. Love to Write is an easy addition to your classroom literacy stations and can involve very little planning. Students benefit from the opportunity to write about something personally meaningful and refine their writing based on the skills they are learning in writing lessons. Another simple tweak is looking for opportunities for your students to share their writing or process. Celebrating this in partners and seeking feedback from each other creates a culture of growth mindset and learning as a process. When students share with a small group or the whole class, it also helps other students see the writing process (and ideas) in action.

Learning from My Mistakes

Love to Write has gone through multiple iterations before it arrived where it is now. Initially, I worked tirelessly to find writing prompts that would excite my students. A new prompt would appear on our Love to Write bulletin board each week. I had a weekly prompt for lists, recipes, and nonfiction, and a picture of the week. Only one or two students would use the prompts each week, yet I would spend tons of time looking for ideas. I realized the time I invested as a teacher needed to translate into student benefit. Also, as in Love to Read, when students would finish Love to Write, they would quickly move on to the next station without a pause. This was a missed opportunity for students to check in with each other about their writing. It was also a missed opportunity for me to check in with students who needed extra accountability or assistance.

Another common mistake in Love to Write is creating too much structure (this might seem counter-intuitive, especially coming from a person who loves structure and control). However, too much structure can stifle the purpose of Love to Write. Students' engagement in topics that are personally meaningful to them is one of the critical motivating factors in the success of this station. The more students can find things they are interested in writing about, the more invested they will be in their writing.

Lastly, in the beginning, I rarely talked to my students about the writing they were doing in Love to Write, and this was a missed opportunity. Having a five-minute (or less) conversation with students about their writing and their personal writing goals allows me to feel confident that I am moving students forward in their learning. Having students show me their writing also shows accountability for how they spend their time at the writing station.

Tweak/Toss/Treasure

Tweak

- What is something you are already doing in your classroom writing instruction that you could adjust slightly to make it more effective? What mentor texts do you love that you could use for reading and writing lessons?

Toss

- What is a belief or practice about teaching students writing that no longer serves you?

Treasure

- What can you take from what has been shared in this chapter and apply to your classroom? What is one small thing you can try that will significantly affect your students' writing (and beliefs about themselves as writers)?

Writing Self-Assessment

Name: ______________________________ Date: ____________________

Writing Goals	My Self-Assessment	My Peer Assessment
I can…		
I can…		
I can…		
I can…		
I can…		
I can…		
I can…		

Pembroke Publishers ©2025 *Making Time for It All* by Kristi Cooper ISBN 978-1-55138-374-3

"Text" Books

Copy this

Dear ______,

"Message Me" — a special notebook where I write messages to you, and you write back!

How it works:

1. I'll write you a note, question, or message.
2. You read it and write back in this book.
3. We keep the conversation going—just like texting, but on paper!
4. **If I make a mistake in my spelling or grammar, that's okay!** You can kindly model the correct spelling or sentence in your message back to me. Writing back and forth helps me build confidence, grow as a reader and writer, and discover the joy of written conversations!

Let's have fun, share stories, ask questions, and write back and forth!

7

Time with Teacher

Finding time to work with students individually or in small groups can be a challenge. Together, we'll explore how literacy stations can create valuable opportunities to meet with students and teach skills tailored to their specific needs. The Time with Teacher station allows educators to provide targeted support, helping students develop the reading and writing skills they need to advance in their learning and growth. It provides valuable opportunities to work with students individually or in small groups. This dedicated time in your daily schedule ensures all learners receive targeted instruction and practice, focusing on the specific skills they need to grow and succeed. At the same time, it provides you with an opportunity to better meet the needs of all of your students.

The other school memory (see page 40) I have related to shame has to do with learning assistance. I struggled with reading and writing in my early years, and I distinctly remember being pulled from class to receive extra support. I had an incredible learning assistance teacher and I liked her, but missing out on the class's activities, as well as learning skills that often didn't translate into the things in the classroom, was difficult. To this day, I can envision the classroom we worked in and the sense of dread I had at being labeled by having to be pulled out for extra help.

Even though learning support and the stigma have changed over the years, I was reluctant as a teacher to have my students miss learning in my classroom to receive extra support. Often, the support felt disjointed, and I didn't feel like I had control over my students' learning. When I moved into the student support role myself, I struggled with this, and looked for other ways to support the needs of students in their reading and writing inside the classroom. While some students still need extra outside support, wherever possible, supporting students in their diverse abilities inside the classroom is most effective (Brownlie, Feniak, & Schnellert, 2016; Moore, 2016).

Over the years, one of my greatest challenges was finding time to work with students on either side of the "norm" in my classroom. I left each day feeling like I was letting down two groups of students: those who needed extra support and those who needed extension in their learning. Day after day, year after year, my lessons were tailored to the majority, and I hoped that, by some miracle, I could get to those who needed extra once in a while.

When I began literacy stations in my classroom, one of the four blocks was Guided Reading. This was my first exposure to doing guided reading with my students and, in many ways, it answered a decade-long problem I had with needing more time to read with my students and work on skills they needed. I played around with different structures for this station and ways that it could work best for my students, and I found that having time to read with small groups of students gave me essential information about how they were doing and what skills they needed to learn to improve. I loved my time with students, but I often wrestled with how best to use that time. If I had students take turns reading, the rest of the students seemed to be disengaged. Yet, the pros outweighed the cons, and I had found a new strategy that helped me feel more successful at meeting my students' needs. Reading with my students in small groups became a priority, and both myself (and the classroom teacher) ran guided reading stations. This meant that our students were being read to consistently, and we saw drastic improvements in student reading.

Every child, every day, needs to read something accurately.

There were still challenges: we were reading with all students for the same amount of time; we had to group students homogeneously; and the time was set and structured, regardless of whether we needed it. With all this in mind, I adjusted our Time with Teacher station to better accommodate a variety of needs and smaller groups of students, and be more responsive to classroom needs.

For me, Time with the Teacher is the highest priority of this literacy station framework. The independent practice of specific skills is essential and necessary, yet the time with the teacher to work on specific and student-centred skills is priceless. Teaching a room full of students who are diverse, with varying needs, isn't for the faint of heart, and finding time to meet all their needs feels like an impossible task. When in peak performance, literacy stations allow teachers to meet with individuals or small groups of students on specific learning goals.

A significant body of research supports the effectiveness of small-group reading and writing instruction (Allington, 2011; Graham & Harris, 2018; Fitzgerald & Shanahan, 2000). However, there are important considerations to ensure that time with students is used effectively and efficiently. Small-group reading and writing instruction is most effective when targeted to the student's specific needs. Students benefit from explicit instruction around the skills they need and benefit from targeted practice when working with the teacher. Small-group (or individual) reading practice significantly improves students' reading fluency, comprehension, and decoding skills and, when done consistently, can significantly improve students' reading ability. Small-group reading and writing practice also enables teachers to work on specific skills that might be areas of concern (the student is missing a few building blocks) or need for extension (the student is ready for learning beyond classroom instruction).

The Time with Teacher station's purpose is to respond to student needs and work with students on the skills that they need to grow in their reading and writing skills. This is a wonderful opportunity to explicitly teach students in areas they might be missing and provide them with intentional and systematic instruction and practice. One-on-one or small-group instruction provides students with opportunities to target skills.

Differentiated instruction for a large number of diverse students is a challenge. Whole-class instruction provides foundational skills that all students need to know. However, it misses the specific needs of students who need extension or support. Time with Teacher allows teachers to work specifically with students on the skills that they need to be individually and systematically taught. Time with

Teacher ensures that we, as educators, can spend intentional, directed time with our students, supporting them in the skills they need the most.

In the Classroom

In Mr Lee's Grade 2 classroom, stations are well underway. As soon as the students settle in, he calls two students, Linden and Avery, over to the Time with Teacher station. In their classroom, Mr. Lee has a heart lamp he turns on when it is uninterrupted teacher time. This provides a great visual cue for his students.

The two students are both working on segmenting sounds into words. He has noticed that both students look at the first sound and then guess the rest of the word when they read. Mr Lee has Elkonin boxes at his table as visual cues, with small items for them to push into the sound boxes when decoding words. He puts the word BIG on a whiteboard and models how to push a toy car into each sound box as he says each sound (phoneme): B - I - G, he moves a car into each box, one for each sound. Although both students can easily decode the word *big*, they work on a few simple CVC words to get them used to the process. Mr Lee then puts the word FISH on the whiteboard. He reminds the students to listen for sounds and not count letters. The students practice with the words FISH, CASH, and BATH, and then Mr Lee adds the word CHEAT to his whiteboard. The students listen to each sound he makes as he moves the cars into each sound box: CH-EA-T. They practice with a few other words together, and Mr Lee reminds them of the importance of looking at all the letters and not just guessing after the first letter. Mr Lee brings out two books for the students to read, reminding them of the skills they just practiced. While Linden appears to have caught on and is working independently at reading the text, Mr Lee notices that Avery needs more support, and works quietly alongside them, prompting them with the Elkonin boxes for words they are decoding. He notices that Avery is getting tired, so he congratulates them both on their perseverance, and sends them back to their stations.

Mr Lee calls a small group of three students to the horseshoe table. These students are all working on extending their writing, and Mr Lee is taking this opportunity to work with them on adding dialogue to their writing. He shows on the whiteboard how to add quotation marks around the words the character is speaking. They read together through a short story and look for places where the author uses dialogue to add interest for the reader. Although the class still needs to learn about dialogue, these students are ready and eager to add it to their writing. The students bring out their writing folders and add some dialogue to a recent piece of writing. Mr Lee checks them over, makes a few corrections, gives encouragement, and then sends them back to their station work.

With only a few minutes left, Mr. Lee looks at his list of students and notices that he hasn't connected with Georgia yet this week. Georgia can decode with proficiency, but she is still emerging in comprehension. Mr Lee chooses a text that is at a more emergent reading level (and easy for Georgia to decode), and they work together to slow down and think while they read. Mr Lee prompts her to check for understanding, and says that if they realize at the end of the page they don't fully understand what is going on, they should go back and reread. They read a few pages together and practice.

Mr Lee records what he worked on with each student and their progress. He makes a few quick comments about how Avery still needs additional support on sounding out words that have vowel teams or blends at the beginning of the words, and makes a note to see her by herself next time.

Literacy Station

Organization

In many frameworks for literacy instruction or stations, the time with teacher is built into the rotation itself, allowing a teacher to strategically meet with every student as they rotate through their station; however, it causes a few key issues as a result. For this to work effectively, students are often grouped by needs or based on reading level or ability. This causes challenges, as it often means all the emerging students are placed in the same group. Behaviorally and for independence, this rarely works. Additionally, your time with students depends on the effective running of the stations and students' stamina. Lastly, the number of students you work with is defined by the group size, not the student needs.

When the Time with Teacher station is removed from the station rotation to become a station of its own, you can pull students responsively into whatever group size you need. Students can be pulled one-on-one, for students who have different needs from others in their classroom, and can be with you at the Time with Teacher station for as long as they are working and learning.

Blood, Barf, or Fire

Once the rest of the stations are running smoothly, Time with Teacher is introduced to students. Introducing this station is always a lot of fun, as I make the guidelines for this station rather dramatic. I share with students that this station is my most treasured and that I look forward to this time with them all week. In my introduction, we talk about growth mindset and how we are all working on different skills as students to help us improve, and at this station, we get to work for a short amount of time on the learning that is just right for us. I introduce how treasured this time is and that it isn't to be interrupted unless there are emergencies.

I am not sure when (or why) the phrase "Blood, Barf, or Fire" was coined, but it has stuck. Students know that the only time they can interrupt the Time with Teacher station is if one of those three things is happening (or about to happen). One of my colleagues added to the phrase and told her students that if Sidney Crosby walks in, they can also interrupt her, so her anchor chart included his photos with the other visuals. Tailoring this limitation on interruption to your own interest and needs makes it both enjoyable and personal.

Teacher Tip
Some teachers have found ways to use visual cues to show their students that Time with Teacher is now active. Night lights, neon signs, or stuffies on desks can all be used to give the class a visual reminder not to interrupt.

Creating a visual for your students to remind them of this hallowed ground can be enjoyable (and silly). However, it continues to remind them of the rules of our class: *I will do my best to learn, and I will help others learn.* As a class, when students see themselves as active and vital members of the community, all helping each other learn, they begin to see the importance of abiding by these guidelines. This is reinforced when students enjoy intentional time with their teacher, and they don't like it to be interrupted.

Modeling with your students what to do when they have a question or need support helps give them strategies to problem-solve when they can't simply rely on asking the teacher. Skills like looking for visual cues around the room, what your peers are doing, and asking a trusted friend are all effective strategies (and lifelong skills) to help students become more independent in their learning and problem-solving.

Personalized Instruction

The Response to Intervention model is a multi-tiered approach to identify and support students' learning needs. When used effectively, it ensures that all students receive the literacy support they need. The RTI model requires teachers to know students' current ability (through assessment) and involves tiered instruction. Tier 1 instruction is defined as high-quality, evidence-based instruction for all students in the classroom (whole-class lessons); Tier 2 instruction is targeted small-group instruction for those students who need extra support beyond Tier 1; and Tier 3 instruction is one-on-one support for those students with significant needs.

Organizing the Time for Teacher station depends on your knowledge of your students and their current state (assessment). Spending time at the beginning of the year on this is essential to its effectiveness. Understanding where your students are in relation to specific skills allows you to support them in what they need to move forward in their learning. Understanding which students need small-group instruction (are developing in the skill but not yet proficient) and those that are emerging (those that need extra support) will guide which students you meet with and how often.

Students who are emerging in specific reading and/or writing skills (phonemic awareness, high-frequency words, comprehension, and fluency) are scheduled for time with the teacher twice as often as those who are proficient. Students who are proficient or extending learners still have goals and skills that they are working on, and they meet with the teacher at least once a week (depending on the number of days and time you run literacy stations). Creating a schedule and keeping track of the goals and skills students are working on allows you to use your time efficiently and effectively.

Once your stations are fully established and your Time with Teacher station is set up and scheduled, you can begin personalized instruction. At this station, you can work with students in small groups or one-on-one, depending on their needs. Because this station operates independently of the station rotations, you can spend as much time as necessary with students while they remain engaged and focused. On some days, you might work with multiple groups or individual students, while, on other days, you might dedicate the entire time to one or two students if their learning requires more attention. The time you spend with each student or group is guided by their learning needs and progress.

Keeping Track of It All

One of the challenges of Time with Teacher in the station rotation is keeping track of which students you have seen and need to see. Planning this proactively avoids problems that can arise if it is left to chance (or memory).

Creating a visual schedule to guide your time ensures that you are responding to the needs of the students in your classroom. There are various ways to organize this, and how you do it is less important than what you include. I have found that having a foundational knowledge of where my students are (in reading and writing) and which skills they are still working on (individual reading and writing goals) or need extra support with helps organize how I spend my time and ensures I am efficient.

What to Do with Extra Adults

Nothing brings me more joy than walking into one of our teachers' classrooms and having them assign me to a station with students. When your Time with Teacher station is outside the rotation of students, it means that, if you have extra adults in your building (learning assistance or support teachers, principals, education assistants), you can utilize them to work with students on specific skills.

If your school has the luxury of having learning support teachers, scheduling them to come into your classroom during station time is an incredible use of their time. On the days they are with you, you can run two Time with Teacher stations. This is a brilliant (and effective) way to show students that all students receive support and that teachers support all students. In my experience, there is often a stigma attached to receiving support from these teachers. Having these teachers work inside the classroom with all students helps "decriminalize" these supports (Moore, 2019). Additionally, educational assistants in your classroom can provide excellent support for students at station practice and can support additional needs.

Using extra adults in your literacy stations reinforces the idea that we are all learning, growing, and needing support. Using your school administration in literacy stations (and in an extra Time with Teacher station) demonstrates to all that learning is a collective and community process. Having your principal come in every once in a while to run a Time with Teacher station can increase not just the number of students you can work with, but can also reinforce the "awesomeness" for students of being able to work with an adult on reading and writing goals. If this feels unrealistic or unlikely, I will challenge you with one of my dad's favorite lines as I was growing up: "All you have to do is ask."

Reflection is an essential part of effective teaching and learning. At the end of chapters 3 to 7, you have opportunities to reflect on what you've read, your practice, and ways to move forward. Tweak, Toss, Treasure is a reflective practice for teachers, and it works great for kids as well.

Teacher Tweaks

Finding time to meet with students in small groups or one-on-one conferences can seem like a daunting task. Start small—do you have 10–15 minutes a day when your students are working that you can begin to try Time with Teacher? Additionally, organizing your class with a Class at a Glance document that shows where your students are at in reading and writing skills (see pages 20–22 for templates) can be a first step to determining which students you would like to target for small-group instruction and the skills you need to work on. One of my favorite sayings, when I'm taking on new things in classrooms, is, "You can only eat an elephant one bite at a time."

Learning from My Mistakes

My goal for literacy stations was to enable me to spend more time with students who needed extra support. However, I was remiss in my effective use of this time. It wasn't enough to simply read with them or check over their writing. I needed to ensure that this time with my students was intentional, proactive, and explicit. Knowing where my students were in their individual reading and writing skills, and the skills they needed to develop, allowed me to make my time with them more effective. Creating individual reading and writing goals with my students and recording them allowed me to use my time intentionally and use other adults (who knew what the students were working on) when they came into the classroom.

Often, I would read with a group of students and notice things about their reading, but would fail to record it anywhere or make any notes. When it came to report-card writing, I had to rely on my memory (which was much better when I was 25) to write comments about my students. One of my mistakes was not keeping track of students' goals, and also their progress and areas for further development. Having a binder or program on your computer where you can keep track of your time with students is incredibly helpful, ensuring continuity to your time with the student and summarizing their progress at report-card time.

Another mistake I made during Time with Teacher was thinking that I needed 20 minutes for the time to be effective. Over the years, I realized that even a few minutes of intentional and explicit instruction can help students improve. Quick little check-ins and instruction can have a big impact on students' skill development. If you have five minutes, use it.

As in all other stations, setting up expected behaviors and continuously reinforcing them is imperative to a thriving learning environment. If students know they can sneak in a quick question or two while you are working with other students, it will snowball. Relentless consistency is your best friend, and will pay dividends in the long run.

Tweak/Toss/Treasure

Tweak

- What is one slight adjustment you could make to your current small-group instruction to better address the diverse needs of all your learners? What could you introduce to your literacy stations that would allow you to meet with students more effectively individually or in small groups for targeted instruction?

Toss

- What is one approach or belief about small-group instruction within your literacy stations that you feel is no longer effective or relevant?

Treasure

- What strategies or practices in your small-group or individual student instruction do you value highly because they consistently support your learners' success?

8

Organizing, Scheduling, and Troubleshooting

Organizing

Using activities students have practiced in whole-group work is essential to making literacy-station life easier. When students have practiced an activity already, it is easy for them to quickly pick it up and get started during literacy station time. A rule of thumb is that, if they haven't seen and practiced it before, it doesn't go into a station. This saves you from answering the barrage of questions about what to do.

Classroom organization can be a limiting factor for teachers when taking on literacy stations. One of the simplest strategies is using a reusable or zipper bag for each student. Having all their materials in a bag or holder allows students to easily bring their work with them to meet with you. Students' writing folders, station work, and a book (or a few) at their instructional reading level make it easy to work with them efficiently. One or two texts that are at a level the students can decode and make meaning from in their bags allows them to use these texts in multiple ways, practicing comprehension skills, word work, and fluency. Station materials include

- Tracking Sheets or binder of student goals and assessments
- Sticky Notes (to make quick notes about students)
- Instructional Level Texts
- Decodable Texts
- Elkonin Boxes
- Letter Tiles
- Whiteboard

Additionally, having a bin or container that holds your activities for Working with Text and that can be easily accessed by you and your students is also helpful. Whiteboards and sticky notes are easy to access and have countless applications at the Working with Text Station.

Scheduling

When setting my schedule, I start with my literacy times, because I use these to integrate so many other subjects.

Setting a weekly schedule for literacy can be challenging, not the least because each school's schedule is unique. Working around gym times and recess breaks can make it difficult to set your own class schedule. Another important consideration is the grade you are teaching and your class composition. For younger years, you could have shorter blocks for whole-class instruction and shorter station rotations. Intermediate students might be able to sustain attention for longer stretches of whole-class instruction, and the activities for them to practice their learning might benefit from longer station times.

You might have to adjust along the way (in fact, you likely will), as you guess and test which schedule works best for your students. Depending on your preference for how you will run your station rotations, you might allow a shorter time, but more often. A frequent mistake is trying it once and, when it doesn't work the way you were hoping, abandoning the concept. Literacy schedules are a bit like making a recipe: you have to work with the ingredients you have, and it often takes a little practice and refining.

Weekly Schedule

Weekly Schedule: Option One

For reproducible Weekly Schedule options in table form, see pages 109 and 110.

Monday

- Morning Message (20 minutes): Review last week's skill and introduce new word work
- Mentor Text (Reading/Writing Whole-Class Instruction) (20 minutes): Focus on a strategy or skill

- Word Work Practice (10 minutes): Phonics or vocabulary focus
- Literacy Stations (3 rotations, 20 minutes each)
- Reflection and Sharing Learning (5 minutes)

Tuesday

- Morning Message (15 minutes): Reinforce word work or comprehension strategy
- Whole-Class Writing Instruction with Guided Practice (30 minutes): Explicit teaching with scaffolded practice
- Literacy Stations (3 rotations, 20 minutes each)
- Reflection and Sharing Learning (5 minutes)

Wednesday

- Morning Message or Reading Whole-Class Instruction (15 minutes): Introduce comprehension skill (e.g., summarizing, making inferences)
- Word Work Practice (10 minutes): Review focus
- Whole-Class Instruction and Practice (30 minutes): Consolidate reading or writing skills
- Literacy Stations (3 rotations, 20 minutes each)
- Reflection & Sharing Learning (5 minutes)

Thursday

- Morning Message or Targeted Instruction (20 minutes): Fluency or comprehension focus
- Word Work Practice (10 minutes)
- Whole-Class Practice (30 minutes): Scaffolded application of strategies
- Literacy Stations (3 rotations, 20 minutes each)
- Reflection and Sharing Learning (5 minutes)

Friday

- Morning Message or Writing Whole-Class Instruction (20 minutes): Wrap-up the week's focus
- Whole-Class Practice (30 minutes)
- Literacy Stations (3 rotations, 20 minutes each)
- Reflection and Sharing Learning (5–10 minutes)

Weekly Schedule: Option Two

Monday

- Mentor Text: Reading and Writing Lesson (30 minutes)
- Whole-Class Practice (15 minutes)
- Literacy Stations (2 x 20 minutes) + Reflection (5 minutes)

Tuesday

- Whole-Class Instruction: Reading or Writing Lesson (30 minutes)
- Whole-Class Practice (15 minutes)
- Literacy Stations (2 x 20 minutes) + Reflection (5 minutes)

Wednesday

- Whole-Class Instruction: Reading or Writing Lesson (30 minutes)
- Whole-Class Practice (15 minutes)
- Literacy Stations (2 x 20 minutes) + Reflection (5 minutes)

Thursday

- Whole-Class Instruction: Reading or Writing Lesson (30 minutes)

- Whole-Class Practice (15 minutes)
- Literacy Stations (2 x 20 minutes) + Reflection (5 minutes)

Friday
- Whole-Class Instruction: Reading or Writing Lesson (30 minutes)
- Whole-Class Practice (15 minutes)
- Literacy Stations (2 x 20 minutes) + Reflection (5 minutes)

School-Year Schedule

I love the start of a new school year (for us, in Canada, it is in September, right when the cool Fall weather begins). School start-ups are full of hope as we eagerly anticipate our new students. Routines are yet to be established, and we are just beginning to get to know the students in our classrooms. The first few months of school are all about building the foundation of a classroom that will support a structure for learning and engagement to flourish. Getting to know your students' interests, setting routines and expectations, and creating a classroom culture where all students are safe to take risks and make mistakes sets the stage for the rest of the year. The work that is done in these beginning months, although it can sometimes seem tedious, is imperative to the success of the rest of the year.

First two months of school
- Building classroom culture and routines
- Getting to know your students
- Building stamina (reading and writing)
- Reading, writing. and word work assessments
- Structured lessons and practice begins

Next two months
- Introduction of stations as practice
- Modeling of expected behaviors
- For younger students, introducing one station at a time
- Practice at stations (stopping and reminding students of expectations when necessary)
- Once stations are introduced and running smoothly, introduce Time with Teacher station

Rest of the year
- Stations are now up and running (adjust as needed)

Troubleshooting

Integrating literacy stations with whole-class instruction is not without its challenges. Strategies and structures that work one year might not work the same way when new students arrive. Each year, adjustments will need to be made, in order to meet the needs of your current students.

Reluctant readers and writers, students' home-life, and your school community and spaces can all provide challenges. Let's look at ways to proactively respond to these issues, to create opportunities to engage parents and community members, and to form school spaces that help students thrive.

Reluctant Writers

Two of my three children were reluctant writers. My son Sam's reluctance to write taught me many things about writing instruction. It seemed like no matter what I tried with him, he still refused to write. This showed up in the classroom and, year after year, teachers would shrug at parent–teacher conferences and helplessly look to me for answers. Then, in Grade 3, Sam had Mrs O for his teacher. She was a veteran (she retired that year) and writing was her passion. I think she took Sam on as a challenge, and we worked together to find ways to get Sam to write.

I learned a lot from Sam (and I continue to). Sometimes, you will meet a student who challenges you and the things you believe to be true about teaching and learning. Ironically, for me, my three kids have been my best teachers in challenging some of my preconceived notions about teaching and learning. For Sam, motivation and engagement were critical. Mrs O's love for writing inspired Sam, as she was one of the first people to show Sam the connection between reading and writing (Sam was an exceptional reader). When Sam was in Grade 3, I saw a Pinterest board that showed a mom taking pictures of her son's Lego creations and using those as a storyboard for his writing. I thought I would give it a try. This proved to be an excellent motivator for Sam. He created Lego scenes (his sister worked alongside him making a Barbie scene) and I took pictures, and we printed those pictures in a storyboard for him to narrate. He loved it. Finding something he was interested in helped motivate him to write.

Tips for Reluctant Writers

- Start with their interests.
- Motivation and engagement are key. Find something that they are interested in and let them write about it.
- Incorporate play and novelty. Finding ways to incorporate play into the writing process helps encourage reluctant writers. Have them draw or create and take photos to get them writing.
- Scaffold and model the process. Your excitement and interest in writing as a teacher will rub off on your students. Carefully scaffolding the process to ensure that students are clear on the process will help get them started. Providing examples and steps on how to get there will help students know the target they are aiming for.
- Remove the pressure. Lower-stakes writing allows students who want things to be just-so to experiment and explore. Love to Write provides time to just write. Knowing that not all writing needs to be perfect and that writing is a process will help students feel safe to experiment and make mistakes.
- Connect to real-life purpose or people. Writing for an authentic audience or person makes writing meaningful. Finding ways for your students to participate in purposeful writing can help even the most reluctant writers.
- Praise. Praising the process and not the product creates a learning environment where students feel safe to take risks. When students are reinforced for taking risks, trying new things, and writing and refining, instead of for a polished product, they are more willing to take chances and write without expecting it to be "right."
- At the Love to Write station: Having options that are low-stakes, with easy entry points, benefits reluctant writers. Opportunities to write simple lists,

draw cartoons, or write postcards are all activities that encourage reluctant writers.

Students Who Struggle to Work Independently

For literacy stations to work effectively, classroom habits and practices must be taught, practiced, and reinforced. Setting the stage for effective stations involves ensuring that the expectations are clear; when things start unravelling, stopping the stations; reinforcing behavior and expectations; and making sure students have the opportunity to reset and restart. Yet, even with clear expectations and classroom management, at times there is a student or students who struggle to work independently. This lack of independence can have a large (and negative) impact on the effectiveness of stations.

One of the ways to support students' ability to work independently is to build stamina. In certain classes and with certain students, you might have to adjust expectations of how many stations you run, or the length of time students are expected to work independently. Often this can be navigated when students understand the task at hand (and have practiced it during whole-class instruction) and are engaged in the learning (given voice and choice). Additionally, breaking larger tasks into smaller chunks can support students who are working toward independence.

Another thing to try is having these students start at the Time with Teacher station. This provides you with the chance to set expectations with the student and ensure they feel confident with the learning tasks.

Every student is individual and, as for any learning activity, it can take some detective work to determine which activities and structures work best for your students and class. As I stated early in the book, this structure is flexible; it can and should be adapted to meet your individual needs and the needs of your students. Often, this will change year over year, as your class and students change.

Parents

Parent communication can be beneficial in supporting the learners in your classrooms. Parents' understanding of reading and writing is often based on their own educational experiences, positive or negative. These beliefs about literacy can leak out and become echoed in classroom culture. Writing home to parents to share what you are doing in your classroom literacy program and stations and to provide them with guidelines and support can prove beneficial. Often, parents need to be made aware of ways they can support their children.

Reading at Home

Parents are often unsure of how to read with their children. Providing them with easy guidelines on what to do when their child comes to a word they don't know or easy ways to help their child practice comprehension can be very supportive for families. See page 111 for a reproducible Info Sheet for Parents.

Writing at Home

In early generations, spelling was the most critical aspect of writing, and it is still something parents often feel very strongly about. Share with your students' parents that correcting all the words in their children's writing creates a reluctance to take risks. Showing them ways to encourage (and model for) children to write at home can provide extra writing practice for students. See page 112 for a reproducible Info Sheet for Parents.

Car-Ride Literacy

Several years ago, a parent shared with me during a parent–teacher meeting their feeling that they were failing their children in supporting their literacy needs. She explained that she spent most of the time after school in cars driving around to practices and that she felt like she was letting her kids down. As a parent of young kids at the time, I related to the feeling of not doing enough to support my kids (mom guilt is a very real thing), and I started brainstorming ways we could play literacy games in the car with my kids. I sent a list home to my students' parents and had many parents talk about the fun they were having in their cars. See reproducible list of activities on page 113.

Engaging Your School Community

This literacy framework is most effective when used in a whole school or community. If students see literacy learning as a way of being, not just something they have to do, it is more meaningful. Engaging extra adults in your literacy stations and activities creates a narrative that learning and stories are everywhere and are done by everyone. Moving your literacy learning beyond the classroom walls also demonstrates that it is not just a "class" thing.

Guest readers and writers in your classroom can provide an opportunity for students to hear how different voices sound, both as readers and writers. Students also benefit from seeing how literacy is integrated into everything we do and used by all school community members, including

- Invited Guests
- Office Staff
- Grandparents
- School Administrators
- Teachers of Different Grades
- Older Students
- Community Members

School Spaces

In a literacy-rich environment, students see opportunities to learn and grow everywhere. Several years ago I had a chance to visit a variety of schools around my province. When I walked into one elementary school, I was blown away by the feeling of learning in action as soon as I entered. Everywhere I looked, there were opportunities to learn. Quiet corners filled the school in nooks and crannies, including in the school office. There were tables in a variety of spaces that students could use to write, and almost every classroom spilled out of its four walls into hallways and shared learning spaces. Student work was everywhere you looked, and meaningful quotes were splashed across the walls. The library was a happening place. Even over lunchtime, students were everywhere engaged in some sort of learning. I was inspired. The staff had decided to make literacy (and learning) a joint effort, and students saw examples of learning everywhere they looked.

School hallways, weird corners, and common learning areas are excellent places for extra learning spaces. Creating cozy reading nooks all around your school illustrates to students that reading can happen anywhere, at any time, by anyone. Imagine the power of a student walking by at recess and seeing a "grownup" reading in a cozy reading nook.

Using school spaces to highlight student work and celebrate rich texts creates an environment where everyone is seen as a reader and an author. Student work that is easily accessible (and pointed out) by other students gives students exemplars for their writing and furthers the narrative of learning being everywhere.

Weekly Schedule: Option One

Monday	Tuesday	Wednesday	Thursday	Friday
Morning Message (20 minutes): Review last week's skill and introduce new word work	Morning Message (15 minutes): Reinforce word work or comprehension strategy	Morning Message or Reading Whole-Class Instruction (15 minutes): Introduce comprehension skill (e.g., summarizing, making inferences)	Morning Message or Targeted Instruction (20 minutes): Fluency or comprehension focus	Morning Message or Writing Whole-Class Instruction (20 minutes): Wrap-up the week's focus
Mentor Text Reading/ Writing Whole-Class Instruction (20 minutes): Focus on a strategy or skill	Whole-Class Writing Instruction with Guided Practice (30 minutes): Explicit teaching with scaffolded practice	Word Work Practice (10 minutes): Review focus	Word Work Practice (10 minutes)	Whole-Class Practice (30 minutes)
Word Work Practice (10 minutes): Phonics or vocabulary focus.		Whole-Class Instruction and Practice (30 minutes): Consolidate reading or writing skills	Whole-Class Practice (30 min): Scaffolded application of strategies	
Literacy Stations (3 x 20 minutes) + Reflection & Sharing Learning (5 minutes)	Literacy Stations (3 x 20 minutes) + Reflection & Sharing Learning (5 minutes)	Literacy Stations (3 x 20 minutes) + Reflection & Sharing Learning (5 minutes)	Literacy Stations (3 x 20 minutes) + Reflection & Sharing Learning (5 minutes)	Literacy Stations (3 x 20 minutes) + Reflection & Sharing Learning (5–10 minutes)

Pembroke Publishers ©2025 *Making Time for It All* by Kristi Cooper ISBN 978-1-55138-374-3

Weekly Schedule: Option Two

Monday	**Tuesday**	**Wednesday**	**Thursday**	**Friday**
Mentor Text: Reading and Writing Lesson (30 minutes)	Whole-Class Instruction: Reading or Writing Lesson (30 minutes)	Whole-Class Instruction: Reading or Writing Lesson (30 minutes)	Whole-Class Instruction: Reading or Writing Lesson (30 minutes)	Whole-Class Instruction: Reading or Writing Lesson (30 minutes)
Whole-Class Practice (15 minutes)	Whole-Class Practice (15 minutes)	Whole-Class Practice (15 minutes)	Whole-Class Practice (15 minutes)	Whole-Class Practice (15 minutes)
Literacy Stations (2 x 20 minutes) + Reflection (5 minutes)	Literacy Stations (2 x 20 minutes) + Reflection (5 minutes)	Literacy Stations (2 x 20 minutes) + Reflection (5 minutes)	Literacy Stations (2 x 20 minutes) + Reflection (5 minutes)	Literacy Stations (2 x 20 minutes) + Reflection (5 minutes)

Info Sheet for Parents

Learning to read can be a special time with your child. It can also be full of unknowns and some frustrations. Reading is a source of joy and any opportunity that you can make the learning fun (and stress-free) will help.

- Find a comfy spot.
- Find books that your child is interested in.
- Praise effort, perseverance, and taking risks.
- Read to, and with, your child.

Decoding

When your child comes to a word they don't know:

- Give them a moment.
- Prompt them by pointing to the letters in the word and asking, "What sounds do they make?" (e.g., /p/.../a/.../t/).
- Prompt them to look for word families or words they might know to help.
- If they read a word incorrectly, ask them, "Did that make sense?" Tell them, "Say the word slowly, looking at all the sounds."

Fluency

Reread sentences to add expression and practice (you can model this with your child) saying the sentence smoothly.

Comprehension

Before, during, and after reading:

- Talk about your thinking while you read (modeling comprehension).
- Talk about the words and what they mean (building vocabulary).
- Connect to the text, Ask Questions, Talk about what you read.

Info Sheet for Writing at Home

Learning to write is an exciting time for your child. They are beginning to explore language, letters, and sounds. Over the next year, you will see huge growth in their writing. Here are some ways you can support their learning at home.

Things they can write (or tell) about:

- Grocery lists
- Letters to loved ones
- Lists (words they know, things they love, names)
- Journals about their day
- Pictures they can label
- Facts they know
- Greeting cards
- Stories about their interests
- Family stories (you can write them together)
- Hand-made books
- A persuasive text (to convince you of something)

Ways to Support Your Child's Writing

- Beginning writing can look like symbols, lines, or strings of letters. Ask your child to read their writing to you. Encourage their creativity and effort. Praise the process, not the product.
- Encourage the joy of writing. When your child is sounding out words to spell, encourage them to listen to the sounds and what letters make those sounds. Say the word slowly to hear all the sounds.
- Don't worry about the correct spelling or grammar. It is about the practice and the process, not perfection.

Car Ride Literacy Games

The Name Game

"The Name Game" is a great song from Shirley Ellis. She plays around with people's names, which is a fun way of playing with words.

> Let's play the name game.
> Doug, Doug Bo Bug, Banana Fanana Fo Fug, Me My Mo Mug, DOUG

Having your kids play with the letters of names can be a fun and silly way of playing with initial sounds.

I Spy

In a simple variation of I Spy, you can play with sounds instead of colors.

> I spy with my little eye, something that starts with *F*.

This can be extended to word families, rhymes, or ending sounds.

One-Word Story

My kids still love this game. It is simple: one word at a time, you go around the car, building a story. Your kids will have to think about what kind of word needs to come next to make the story make sense: Does a verb, noun, adjective, preposition need to come next in the story? This can provide great laughs as big and little kids try to keep track of the story in their heads and add to it.

License Plate Words

Find a letter on a license plate and come up with as many words as you can that start with that letter.

Rhyme It

Take turns saying a word, and then everyone in the car tries to come up with as many rhyming words as possible until they run out.

I'm going on a picnic, and I'm going to bring…

Each player takes turns being the person who creates the category in their mind. The other members have to guess what the category is. The host starts, "I'm going on a picnic, and I'm going to bring an apple." The next person says, "I'm going on a picnic, and I'm going to bring a banana." The host would say whether or not they could come, based on the rule in their head. If their rule was *words that start with a*, that person could not come; if it was *fruit*, they could. The group keeps trying to bring things to the picnic until they figure out the rule.

Car Ride Literacy Games (cont'd)

Alphabetical Order

Take turns finding words around you (or that you see) alphabetically.

Word Chain

Someone says a word, then the next person uses the last letter to say the next word. You can adjust this to be the last sound for younger kids.

Guess the Word

Think of a word and give clues about its meaning, starting with broader hints and getting more specific until someone guesses it.

Word Construction

Say a word and then explain how to take it apart.

Bright. Repeat it, but leave off the *B*.
Rainbow. Repeat it, but leave off *bow*.
Mad. Repeat it, but leave off the *d*.

Final Thoughts

Writing this book has reminded me of the many people who have shaped my life and career. As I reflected on my own journey as a student, I saw how profoundly teachers influenced my understanding of myself as a learner. During my early teaching years, veteran teachers and remarkable administrators guided and encouraged me as I navigated the often challenging path of a beginning teacher. Now, as a more experienced teacher, I continue to learn alongside colleagues who dedicate themselves to the hard work of teaching in an ever-evolving educational landscape.

When I was in Grade 2, my teacher Mrs. Hamilton inspired me to become a teacher myself. She embodied everything I aspired to be and helped me believe in myself as a learner. Looking back, I realize how much compassion, dedication, and hard work it takes to be a teacher like that.

Teaching is not a job that ends when the school bell rings. Few outside the profession truly understand the emotional, mental, spiritual, and physical effort it demands. Every day, we have the privilege of helping children discover their unique gifts and watching them learn. We nurture their interests and passions, constantly adapting our practice to meet their needs, even as the demands of the curriculum and educational mandates evolve. Despite the challenges, teachers remain resilient, year after year, committed to growing as educators and inspiring their students.

During my first year of teaching, a student gave me a sticker with a poem called "She Who Is Called to Teach." That poem sat on my desk for years, reminding me that teaching is more than just a job, it's a calling. When I took on the role of teacher coach, I aimed to make my colleagues' jobs a little bit easier while reminding them of the incredible work they were doing. In writing this book, I hope to do the same. I hope the insights shared here make your teaching journey just a little bit smoother. Knowing that teachers take time to read this book amid their *countless* responsibilities is humbling.

As we wrap up, here are a few key takeaways:

1. *What's Your Point?* My dad used to ask me this whenever I worked on writing assignments. It's a question that still guides me, whether I'm writing or planning a lesson. Knowing your purpose helps clarify what truly matters, allowing you to focus on meaningful learning and let go of what doesn't serve your goals.

2. *Know Your Ingredients* I often think of my mom's ability to make refrigerator soup, creatively turning leftovers into something delicious. Teaching is similar. Each year brings a new group of students with unique needs, talents, and personalities. The magic lies in knowing your "ingredients" well and working together to create a classroom where all students belong and flourish.
3. *One Bite at a Time* Sometimes, professional development can feel overwhelming, making us think we must change everything at once. Instead, consider adding or tweaking just one aspect of your practice. The suggestions in this book are meant to inspire small, manageable changes that fit your teaching style and context.

Teachers truly are everyday superheroes. You might never fully know the impact you have on your students, but your dedication to creating spaces of belonging and learning makes a difference. I hope, as you read this, you reflect on the educators and people who brought you to where you are now and know that, like them, you are inspiring the next generation of learners.

Glossary

Accuracy: The ability to correctly read and pronounce words without errors. Accuracy is a key component of reading fluency and is essential for comprehension.

Alphabetic Principle: The understanding that written letters (graphemes) correspond to specific spoken sounds (phonemes) in a predictable and systematic way.

Blending: The ability to combine individual sounds (phonemes) or parts of a word to form a complete word.

Decodable Text: Text that is specifically designed to align with phonics instruction, allowing students to practice decoding words based on learned sound-letter relationships.

Decoding: The process of interpreting written words by translating graphemes into their corresponding phonemes and blending them to form a recognizable word.

Elkonin Box: A teaching tool used to build phonemic awareness and segmentation skills. Students use a series of boxes to represent each sound (phoneme) in a word, placing a marker or letter in the appropriate box.

Encoding: The process of converting spoken words into written form by segmenting sounds and using graphemes to represent them.

Etymology: The study of the origin and historical development of words, including how their meanings, forms, and spellings have evolved over time.

Fluency: The ability to read with speed, accuracy, and proper expression (prosody). Fluent readers recognize words automatically, allowing them to focus on comprehension.

Grapheme: The smallest written unit in a language that represents a phoneme. A grapheme can be a single letter (e.g., *b*) or a group of letters (e.g., *sh*).

High-Frequency Words: Commonly used words that appear often in written text. Learning these words supports fluency.

Independent Level: The level at which a student can read and comprehend text comfortably without teacher support; 95–100% of the words are read independently.

Instructional Level: The level at which a student can read with teacher support, demonstrating 90–94% accuracy and adequate comprehension. This level is appropriate for guided reading and scaffolding instruction.

Metacognition: The awareness and regulation of one's own thought processes, especially during reading or learning; thinking about one's thinking. It involves monitoring comprehension and applying strategies to improve understanding.

Morpheme: The smallest unit of meaning in a language. A morpheme may be a root word, prefix, or suffix.

Orthographic Mapping: The cognitive process by which readers store written words in their long-term memory for instant retrieval. It connects the sounds (phonemes), letters (graphemes), and meanings of words, enabling automatic word recognition.

Orthography: The conventional spelling system of a language, including the rules and patterns that govern how words are written.

Phoneme: The smallest unit of sound in a spoken word that distinguishes one word from another.

Phonemic Awareness: The ability to identify, isolate, and manipulate individual sounds (phonemes) in spoken words. It is a subset of phonological awareness and does not involve written text.

Phonics: A method of teaching reading and writing that emphasizes the relationship between letters (graphemes) and sounds (phonemes). Phonics instruction helps students decode words by understanding spelling patterns.

Phonogram: A written symbol (letter or group of letters) that represents a sound or a series of sounds in a word.

Phonological Awareness: A broad skill that includes recognizing and manipulating units of spoken language, such as words, syllables, onsets, and rimes, in addition to individual phonemes. Phonemic awareness is a subset of this larger skill.

Prosody: The rhythm, stress, and intonation of speech in oral reading. It contributes to reading fluency and comprehension by adding expression and natural pacing to the text.

Rhyme: Words that share the same ending sounds from the vowel onward.

Segmenting: The ability to break down words into their individual sounds (phonemes) or syllables. It is a critical phonemic awareness skill.

Professional Resources

Mentor Texts by Theme and Topic

Writing

Books to Teach Ideas

Rocket Writes a Story by Tad Hills
The Idea Jar by Adam Lehrhaupt
Harold and the Purple Crayon by Crockett Johnson
Not a Box by Antoinette Portis

Books to Teach Organization

Diary of a Fly by Doreen Cronin (diary writing)
One Day, The End by Rebecca Kai Dotlich (adding detail)
Roller Coaster by Marla Frazee (story Ssructure)
The Darkest Dark by Chris Hadfield (personal narrative)
Amazing Grace by Mary Hoffman (personal narrative)
Hey, Little Ant by Phillip and Hannah Hoose (persuasive writing)
Neville by Norton James (personal narrative)
Once Upon A Memory by Nina Laden (pattern writing)
Finding Wild by Megan Wagner Lloyd (descriptive writing)
I Will Not Read This Book by Cece Meng (persuasive writing)
If You Give a Mouse a Cookie by Laura Joffe Numeroff (circle stories)
What Does Peace Feel Like? by V. Radunsky (descriptive writing)
I Wish You More by Amy Krouse Rosenthal (pattern writing)
Alpha-Better by Dan Bar-el and Graham Ross (alphabet book)
If Everybody Did by Jo Ann Stover (pattern writing)
Dear Mrs. Larue by Mark Teague (letter writing)
If I Built a House by Chris Van Duesen (how-to writing)

Books to Teach Word Choice

Big Words for Little People by Jamie Lee Curtis
Phileas's Fortune by Agnes De Lestrade
Show, Don't Tell: Secrets of Writing by Josephine Nobisso and Eva Montanari
Words by Lora Rozler

The Boy Who Loved Words by Roni Schotter
The Very Inappropriate Word by Jim Tobin

Books to Teach Sentence Fluency

The Important Book by Margaret Wise Brown
Brave Irene by William Steig
Owl Moon by Jane Yolen

Books to Teach Voice

Voices in the Park by Anthony Brown
Louise Loves Art by Kelly Light

Books to Teach Conventions

How Much Can A Bare Bear Bear? What Are Homonyms and Homophones? by Brian P. Cleary
Happy Endings: A Story About Suffixes by Robin Pulver
Punctuation takes a Vacation by Robin Pulver
Eats, Shoots & Leaves: Why Commas Really Do Make a Difference! by Lynne Truss

Books to Teach Writing Process

The Squiggle Story by Andrew Larson
Ralph Tells a Story by Abby Hanlon
Little Red Writing by Joan Holub
A Perfectly Messed Up Story by Patrick McDonnell
The Best Story by Eileen Spinelli
Help! I Need a Title by Henre Tullet
I Am a Story by Dan Yaccarino

Reading Comprehension

Books to Teach Rhyming

Duck in the Truck by Jez Alborough
A Moment in Time by Jennifer Butenas
Llama Llama Red Pajama by Anna Dewdney
Nothing Rhymes with Orange by Adam Rex
Sheep in a Jeep by Nancy E. Shaw

Books to Teach Summarizing

Enemy Pie by Derek Munson
Martin's Big Words: The Life of Dr. Martin Luther King, Jr. by Doreen Rappaport and Bryan Collier
A Bad Case of Stripes by David Shannon
Knuffle Bunny by Mo Willems
Four Feet, Two Sandals by Karen Lynn Williams, Khadra Mohammed, et al.
The Other Side by Jacqueline Woodson

Nonfiction Story Books

Weeds Find a Way by Cindy Jenson-Elliott
Over and Under the Snow by Kate Messner
Sophie's Squash by Pat Zietlow Miller and Anne Wilsdorf
Lifetime by Lola M. Schaefer

Books to Teach Figurative Language

My Mouth Is a Volcano by Julia Cook
Click, Clack, Moo: Cows that Type by Doreen Cronin and Betsy Lewin
The Legend of Rock Paper Scissors by Drew Daywalt
My Dog Is as Smelly as Dirty Socks: And Other Funny Family Portraits by Hanoch Piven
I Am Peace: A Book of Mindfulness (I Am Books) by Susan Verde and Peter H. Reynolds

Books to Teach Question Asking

Zoom by Istvan Banyai
Fly Away Home by Eve Bunting
The Uncorker of Ocean Bottles by Michelle Cuevas
The Girl with Big, Big Questions by Britney Winn Lee
The Stranger by Chris Van Allsburg

Books to Teach Visualizing

Fireflies by Julie Brinckloe
The Black Book of Colors by Menena Cottin
Jessie's Island by Sheryl McFarlane
I Hear a Pickle by Rachel Isadora
Listening Walk by Paul Showers

Books to Teach Inference

Hug by Jez Alborough
Hello! Hello! by Matthew Cordell
How to Heal a Broken Wing by Bob Graham
Sidewalk Flowers by JonArno Lawson
Float by Daniel Miyares

Books to Teach Author's Purpose

Rosie Revere, Engineer by Andrea Beaty
The Girl Who Thought in Pictures by Julia Finley Mosca
Last Stop on Market Street by Matt de la Pena

Books to Teach Point of View

The Bad Seed by Jory John
We Found a Hat by Jon Klassen
This Very Tree: A Story of 9/11, Resilience, and Regrowth by Sean Rubin
After the Fall by Dan Santat
The True Story of the Three Little Pigs by Jon Scieszka
They All Saw a Cat by Brendan Wenzel

Books to Teach Theme

Those Shoes by Maribeth Boelts
One Green Apple by Eve Bunting
Spaghetti on a Hot Dog Bun by Maria Dismondy
Red: A Crayon's Story by Michael Hall
Spork by Kyo Maclear
A Bad Case of Stripes by David Shannon

References and Recommended Reading

Allington, R. L. (2012). "Every Child, Every Day" *Educational Leadership, 69*(6), 10–15.

Allington, R. L. (2011). *What Really Matters for Struggling Readers: Designing research-based programs.* North York, ON: Pearson.

Boaler, J. (2016). *Mathematical Mindsets: Unleashing students' potential through creative math, inspiring messages and innovative teaching.* Hoboken, NJ: Jossey-Bass.

Boaler, J. (2019). *Limitless Mind: Learn, lead, and live without barriers.* San Francisco, CA: HarperOne.

Boushey, G., & Moser, J. (2006). *The Daily Five: Fostering literacy independence in the elementary grades.* Portland, ME: Stenhouse Publishers.

British Columbia Ministry of Education. (n.d.). *English language arts curriculum: K-9.* https://curriculum.gov.bc.ca/

British Columbia Ministry of Education. (2023). *Early learning framework: From birth to age eight.* British Columbia Ministry of Education. https://www2.gov.bc.ca/assets/gov/education/early-learning/teach/earlylearning/early_learning_framework.pdf

Brownlie, F, (2015). *Grand Conversations, Thoughtful Responses.* Winnipeg, MB: Portage & Main Press.

Brownlie, F., & Schnellert, L. (2009). *It's All About Thinking: Collaborating to support all learners in English, social studies, and humanities.* Winnipeg, MB: Portage & Main Press.

Brownlie, F., Feniak, C., & Schnellert, L. (2016). *Student Diversity: 3rd Edition, Classroom strategies to meet the learning needs of all students.* Markham, ON: Pembroke Publishers.

Burkins, J., & Yates, K. (2021). *Shifting the Balance: 6 ways to bring the science of reading into the balanced literacy classroom.* Portland, ME: Stenhouse Publishers.

Calkins, L. (1986). *The Art of Teaching Writing.* Portsmouth, NH: Heinemann.

Cauley, K. M., & McMillan, J. H. (2010). "Formative Assessment Techniques to Support Student Motivation and Achievement" *The Clearing House: A Journal of Educational Strategies, Issues and Ideas, 83*(1), 1–6. Retrieved from https://drakeinstitute.osu.edu

Christakis, D. A., Zimmerman, F. J., DiGiuseppe, D. L., & McCarty, C. A. (2004). "Early Television Exposure and Subsequent Attentional Problems in Children" *Pediatrics, 113*(4), 708–713.

Cohen, B., & Chambers, N. (Eds.). (2016). *M'ym'aytwixwmntm IƗ Sqilxwtət: Stories of our Sqilxw ways.* Vernon. BC: Okanagan Indian Band.

Culham, R. (2003). *6+1 Traits of Writing: The complete guide for teachers* (2nd ed.). Toronto, ON: Scholastic.

Culham, R. (2018). *6+1 traits of writing: The complete guide for the primary grades.* Toronto, ON: Scholastic.

Culham, R. (2014). *The Writing Thief: Using mentor texts to teach the craft of writing.* Portland, ME: Stenhouse Publishers.

Cunningham, P. M., & Hall, D. P. (1998). *The Four Blocks: A balanced framework for literacy in primary classrooms.* Brookline, MA: Brookline Books

Duke, N. K., & Cartwright, K. B. (2021). *"The Science of Reading Progresses: Communicating advances beyond the simple view of reading" Reading Research Quarterly, 56*(S1), S25–S44. https://doi.org/10.1002/rrq.411

Dweck, C. (2014, November). *The power of yet* [Video]. TEDx. https://www.ted.com/talks/carol_dweck_the_power_of_yet

Ehri, L. C. (2022). "What Teachers Need to Know and Do to Teach Letter–sounds, Phonemic Awareness, Word Reading, and Phonics" *The Reading Teacher, 76*, 53–61. https://doi.org/10.1002/trtr.2095

First Nations Education Steering Committee. (n.d.). *First Peoples Principles of Learning.* https://www.fnesc.ca/first-peoples-principles-of-learning/

Fitzgerald, J., & Shanahan, T. (2000). "Reading and Writing Relations and their Development" *Educational Psychologist, 35*(1), 39–50.

Florida Center for Reading Research. (2009). *Guidelines for Reading Intervention and Literacy Block Scheduling.* Florida Center for Reading Research. https://www.fcrr.org

Fountas, I., & Pinnell, G. S. (2018). "Every Child, Every Classroom, Every Day: From vision to action in literacy learning" *The Reading Teacher, 72*(1), 7–19.

Fuchs, L. S., & Fuchs, D. (2006). "Progress Monitoring in RTI: Frequently asked questions" *The Reading Teacher, 58*(3), 188–192. https://doi.org/10.1598/RT.58.3.5

Gallagher, K. (2011). *Write Like This: Teaching Real-world Writing through Modeling & Mentor Texts.* Portland, ME: Stenhouse Publishers.

Gambrell, L. B. (2011). "Seven Rules of Engagement: What's most important to know about motivation to read" *The Reading Teacher, 65*(3), 172–178. https://doi.org/10.1002/TRTR.01024

Gear, A. (2008). *Reading Power: Teaching Students to Think while they Read.* Markham, ON: Pembroke Publishers.

Gear, A. (2015). *Powerful Understanding: Helping Students Explore, Question, and Transform their Thinking about Themselves and the World Around Them.* Markham, ON: Pembroke Publishers.

Gear, A. (2011). *Writing Power: Engaging Thinking through Writing.* Markham, ON: Pembroke Publishers.

Gough, P. B., & Tunmer, W. E. (1986). "Decoding, Reading, and Reading Disability" *Remedial and Special Education, 7*(1), 6–10.

Graham, S., & Hebert, M. A. (2010). *Writing to Read: Evidence for how writing can improve reading.* A Carnegie Corporation Time to Act Report. Washington, DC: Alliance for Excellent Education.

Graham, S., Harris, K. R., & Santangelo, T. (2015). "Research-based Writing Practices and the Common Core: Meta-analysis and meta-synthesis" *The Elementary School Journal, 115*(4), 498–522. https://doi.org/10.1086/681964

Graves, D. H. (2003). *Writing: Teachers and children at work* (20th anniversary ed.). Portsmouth, NH: Heinemann.

Guthrie, J. T., & Wigfield, A. (2000). "Engagement and Motivation in Reading" In M. L. Kamil, P. B. Mosenthal, P. D. Pearson, & R. Barr (Eds.), *Handbook of reading research* (Vol. 3, pp. 403–422). Mahwah, NJ: Lawrence Erlbaum Associates.

International Literacy Association. (2018). *Explaining the "Science of reading": Independent reading and the K–3 literacy block.* Newark, DE: International Literacy Association. https://www.literacyworldwide.org

Johnston, P. H. (2004). *Choice Words: How our Language Affects Children's Learning.* Portland, ME: Stenhouse Publishers.

Kelly, J. (2023). *Active Reading Classrooms: Strategies that Build Language Comprehension and Word Recognition Skills.* Markham, ON: Pembroke Publishers.

Kilpatrick, D. A. (2015). *Essentials of Assessing, Preventing, and Overcoming Reading Difficulties.* Hoboken, NJ: John Wiley & Sons.
K12 Reader. (2018). "The Relationship Between Reading and Writing." Retrieved from K12 Reader https://www.k12reader.com/the-relationship-between-reading-and-writing/
Ladson-Billings, G. (1995). "Toward a Theory of Culturally Relevant Pedagogy" *American Educational Research Journal, 32*(3), 465–491. https://doi.org/10.3102/00028312032003465
Lewis, K. (2018). "Lessons Learned: Applying principles of reading recovery in the classroom" *The Reading Teacher, 71*(6), 727–734.
Liljedahl, P. (2020). *Building Thinking Classrooms in Mathematics: 14 Teaching Practices for Enhancing Learning.* Thousand Oaks, CA: Corwin.
Marzano, R. J., & Marzano, J. S. (2003). "Building Classroom Relationships" *Educational Leadership, 61*(1), 6–13. Retrieved from https://www.ascd.org
Mielonen, A. M., & Paterson, W. (2009). "Developing Literacy through Play" *Journal of Inquiry & Action in Education*, 3(1), 15-27.
Miller, D. (2009). *The Book Whisperer: Awakening the Inner Reader in Every Child.* Hoboken, NJ: Jossey-Bass.
Moore, S. (2016). *One Without the Other: Stories of unity through diversity and inclusion.* Winnipeg, MB: Portage & Main Press.
Moore, S. (2019, January 17). *Transforming Inclusive Education* [Video]. YouTube. https://www.youtube.com/watch?v=RYtUlU8MjlY
National Institute of Child Health and Human Development. (2000). *Report of the National Reading Panel: Teaching Children to Read: An evidence-based assessment of the scientific research literature on reading and its implications for reading instruction.* (NIH Publication No. 00-4769). U.S. Government Printing Office. https://www.nichd.nih.gov/sites/default/files/publications/pubs/nrp/Documents/report.pdf
Novak, K. (2022). *UDL now! A Teacher's Guide to Applying Universal Design for Learning* (3rd ed.). Chicago, IL: CAST Professional Publishing.
Pearson, P. D., & Gallagher, M. C. (1983). "The Instruction of Reading Comprehension" *Contemporary Educational Psychology, 8*(3), 317–344. https://doi.org/10.1016/0361-476X(83)90019-X
Politano, C., & Paquin, J. (2000). *Brain-based Learning with Class.* Winnipeg, MB: Portage & Main Press.
Reutzel, D. R., & Cooter, R. B. (2005). *The Essentials of Teaching Children to Read: What Every Teacher Needs to Know.* North York, ON: Pearson.
Scarborough, H. S. (2001). "Connecting Early Language and Literacy to Later Reading (Dis)Abilities: Evidence, theory, and practice" In S. Neuman & D. Dickinson (Eds.), *Handbook of early literacy research* (pp. 97–110). New York, NY: Guilford Press.
Schmoker, M. (2019). "The Problem with Literacy Programs" *Education Week.* Summarized in *Marshall Memo, 776.*
Sedita, J. (2023). *The Writing Rope: A Framework for Explicit Writing Instruction in All Subjects.* Baltimore, ML: Brookes Publishing.
Serravallo, J. (2015). *The Reading Strategies Book: Your Everything Guide to Developing Skilled Readers.* Portsmouth, NH: Heinemann.
Serravallo, J. (2017). *The Writing Strategies Book: Your Everything Guide to Developing Skilled Writers.* Portsmouth, NH: Heinemann.
Such, C. (2021). *The Art and Science of Teaching PrimaryRreading.* Thousand Oaks, CA: Sage Publications

Vygotsky, L. S. (1978). *Mind in Society: The Development of Higher Psychological Processes.* Cambridge, MA: Harvard University Press.

Wolf, M. (2019). "The Science and Poetry in Learning (and Teaching) to Read" *Phi Delta Kappan, 100*(4), 13–17.

Zimmerman, B. J. (2002). "Becoming a Self-regulated Learner: An overview" *Theory Into Practice, 41*(2), 64–70. https://doi.org/10.1207/s15430421tip4102_2

Zimmerman, B. J., & Schunk, D. H. (2011). *Self-regulated Learning and Academic Achievement: Theoretical Perspectives* (2nd ed.). Milton Park, UK: Routledge. https://doi.org/10.4324/9780203831076

Index